Doing Time in "Q"

The Story of One Man's Life in Prison

Margery Ada McAleer

Eloquent Books

Eloquent Books
An imprint of Strategic Book Group
P.O. Box 333
Durham CT 06422
www.StrategicBookGroup.com

ISBN:978-1-60860-439-5

Printed in the United States of America

Book Design: Suzanne Kelly

In memory of my father, Lt. Dan Coughlin, aka The Loot, whose life inspired this story.

Prologue

January 1926

Evening had descended on the prison as flickering shadows played across the stone walls of the cellblock, creating an eerie collage of dark images like wavering actors on a shifting stage for the young prisoner standing within the small yellow-chalked circle. It had been over an hour and the usual punishments always ran in four-hour shifts or until the guard tired. At least, that's what the old timers had told him. Somewhere a whistle blew. *A train whistle?* The prisoner staggered, then straightened. *No, there were no trains in hell,* he thought, shaking his head. Staring over at the row of cells, he couldn't see their eyes but knew they were over there appraising him. Once again he attempted to hold his head high despite the excruciating pain that traveled along his spine and expanded across his chest like a boa constrictor, squeezing the very life from his body.

"Jesse," His mother's voice seemed hollow, echoing like she was at the bottom of a well. "You get home now!"

Trying to answer, his voice was too weak, almost paralyzed in its tomb and he had to swallow hard, croaking, *"Comin' Ma!"* He tried to run to her but his legs wouldn't move. *Had the heat been turned higher,* he wondered, and wished the sweat soaking his body would dry-up so he could stop shivering.

Swaying, he again struggled to keep a balance but his nose now started dripping. The effort in raising an arm to wipe it with his sleeve would result in movement and stepping outside the circle would bring more painful floggings with the rubber garden hose. That stung all to hell! Even shifting feet could bring a cascade of whippings with that hose tearing the shirt, chewing his flesh, bruising and breaking ribs. With jaw stubbornly set and teeth clamped down hard on the tongue, he staggered, falling to his knees, head bent in prayerful supplication just as a guard approached, footsteps resounding along the cellblock tier.

Feeling the cutting sting of the whip across his back almost before it struck like a coiled snake, hissing again and again, he almost welcomed the pain and numbness washing over his body because it meant the end of the ordeal. Or did it? Despite the blood oozing from his nose and mouth while drawing a tortured breath, his heart soared. In these last conscious moments he was thankful that even while the lashings brought smarting tears to his closed eyes, they never rolled down his face. The old timers would be surprised that the young squirt who had been the object of so much ridicule since his first day, had some guts, after all. They would never know the agonizing price he was paying for those few proud moments.

"Shove him into a cell," the rotund guard barked as a prisoner rushed over and dragged the dying man toward a cell. "I'll report that he tried to escape before we haul him over to the infirmary in the morning, if he's still alive."

Looking around the cellblock into the dark well where hundreds of unseen eyes were glued upon the scene, he shouted, "Anyone here got a different story?"

After slamming the heavy doors leading from the cellblock, the guard failed to hear the tap, tap, tap, tapping of tin cups on the bars, which gradually grew into a loud crescendo, then stopped as abruptly as it began when another guard walked into the cellblock.

Suddenly, a scream cut across the silent cells and a voice rose from the darkness, yelling, "Jeessus! He bit off his own tongue. Jeessus! How'd he do that?"

As the sobbing persisted, echoing in the cellblock, the angry men remained in stony silence. Only an occasional curse rose from the cell where the dying prisoner, vomiting blood and shivering in shredded skin, was being tended by cellmates. His death would later be attributed to an unsuccessful attempt to escape over the walls of the prison. There had always been ugly rumors circulating throughout the cellblocks that one end of the whipping hose was filled with lead pellets. Other prisoners also claimed that one of the guards known by some of the men as Walrus and by others as Handlebars, carried brass knuckles cleverly concealed inside a thick leather glove on one hand.

"Won't touch them dirty skins with my own hands, you betcha," Walrus would say, loud enough to be overheard by an entire cellblock.

Chapter I

San Francisco
March 1926

S itting in Peadar Collins' home perched high on a stiff-necked hill with sweeping views, Dan Grady stared through windows freckled with water stains, across empty blowing sand dunes stretching toward the Pacific Ocean. The sun had spread an orange marmalade sliding across the blue waters.

"You have a great place here, Paddy."

"Aye, Danny, but it's not home." Peadar, also known as Paddy, was a wiry man with a hedgeful of cropped white hair who had fled during the 1916 Uprisings in Ireland when his comrades were being arrested and imprisoned by the British. Some of these men had even opted for starvation in prison before acknowledging defeat.

"I never thought for one minute that we would succeed." Paddy said, shaking his head while sipping the whiskey and nervously running a hand through his quill-like hair.

Still harboring the guilt of one considered a brother rat by imprisoned friends Paddy spent a considerable amount of time explaining his sudden departure from the ragtag army of rebels.

"America took me in, a true Irish orphan, Danny, and I will forever be indebted, but you know, my heart is buried over there." He spoke softly, blue eyes squinting as though looking into a distant time through the curtain of years, while they sat in the small kitchen sipping whiskey and gazing at the glass-sculptured sea.

Paddy had adopted America as rapidly as a newborn finds its mother's breast. He proudly wore an American flag pin on his lapel, hung the flag on his porch every holiday including Christmas and always stood stiffly saluting whenever the Star Spangled Banner was played.

"I know," Paddy lamented. "After all these years, the situation still looks hopeless." Clicking his tongue and for a moment he was swept back in memory to another time as he said, "At least in this country, there's a future for us."

Bitter-sweet memories in Dan's mind were buried so deeply that excavation would not only be too painful but would result in tearing open old crusted scabs. Dan lit a cigarette, tossing the match into an ashtray and taking a deep drag on the Camel, said, "I seldom reflect on those terrible years, Paddy. It was a waste of so many lives pursuing that dream of freedom and, when you think of it, waging a battle with hayforks, shovels and hard-knuckled fists as our only weapons against guns and armored tanks."

Shaking his head forlornly, Dan looked beyond his friend toward the horizon as if searching for an answer within the blue waters as his thoughts dropped back in time. The hard stones used for pillows when the line of men paused to sleep alongside a dusty road; the scent of freshly-mown hay blanketing cold bodies as they slept on those forays; the aroma of thick black foamy ale wafting from the small pubs they passed on their marches through Cork and, above all, the loved ones resting forever under tombstones, were memories Dan had stored until some day in the future when he could open the album in his mind, remove each snapshot, one by one, and then maybe the tears would come.

Studying Dan, a tall, fair-skinned man with faded blue eyes, strong chin and prematurely white hair, Paddy said, "I hope this new start will give you some peace of mind, Danny." When his friend did not respond, Paddy sighed and turned away, saying,

"What do you remember of that terrible day inside that prison, Danny?"

Startled by the question, Dan set his glass on the table, saying, "You mean after you went over the wall?"

Now on the defensive, Paddy's face tightened with concern and in an almost pleading voice, "Ah, Danny. I couldn't take it anymore."

"I understand," Dan said, nodding and sipping the whiskey. "Not many could take it, Paddy. They're all buried somewhere inside those walls."

Seeing the haunted look in his friend's eyes, Paddy decided the air was pulsating with too many dark memories to pursue the conversation any farther and he rose from the chair, saying, "Let's put all that behind us now and drink to the future. And there's a great one for you. I remember how well you worked with those poor lads in the prison over there. So when I heard of this opening from my old friend, the prison chaplain, I knew just who to call." His eyes narrowed as he studied Dan's reaction. "You know, for the Probation Department, I'm in daily contact with men being paroled from prison and, believe me, Danny, some men aren't ready to return to society. Jeessus! Most will swear they'll go straight and then, Jesus, Mary and Joseph! I'm out there looking for them in a month. Sure enough, there's my sticky-fingered ex-con plundering my grocer. There's nothing being done to prepare them for a return to society." He turned to gaze through the windows. "I'm so damned sick of this situation. There must be something we can do, Danny."

As Paddy stood and reached for the bottle of Irish whiskey, his jacket fell open, revealing green trademark suspenders with shamrocks brightly scrolled along them.

"Sure, you haven't changed at all Paddy. Still thumbing your nose at the English?"

"Oh, yeah, Danny, my suspenders! The trouble is that people here don't even recognize my favorite posy. Why, I've been asked if they weren't four-leaf clovers. Can you imagine?"

"I suppose, in a way, that's good, Paddy."

The light moment soon passed as they finished drinking the rich fluid and Paddy, capping the bottle, placed it on a shelf till the next time. Dan rose and removing his coat from the back of the chair, carefully smoothed the lapels before he shrugged into it and said, "Those prison conditions were so terrible. They killed more of our boys through disease and starvation than with bullets, that's for sure."

"I know, Danny." Paddy looked keenly into his friend's face. "I don't know that I can say the prison conditions here are much better."

"Really? And what's wrong with them?"

"Well, there's talk of medieval practices which many prison officials deny, insisting that the floggings ended years ago. They admit the dungeon exists but it's rarely used and then only for incorrigibles. Perhaps after you get inside as an employee, you'll be able to see if it's true."

"I don't know, Paddy. If that's true, what could I do about it?"

"You helped over there, Danny. By protesting loudly, you were able to get them medical help."

"Well, you know who that was?"

"Of course, but veterinarians were better than nobody. At least they had some knowledge of the animal body, whether horse or man. Your apprenticeship with Saemus O'Flarity was the best thing you ever did for yourself, Danny."

"He was a great veterinarian and admirer of fine horseflesh. He was a loss to Ireland when he died in that filthy prison."

"He was executed there, Paddy. Remember?"

While Dan spoke, Paddy was remembering how Dan's large capable hands had not only changed many dressings on injured men, held the reins of protesting horses while being shod and tenderly coddled a new foal, still wrapped in its mother's blood.

"I'm glad you decided to come over to this country, Danny, even if raiding Stills wasn't your idea of a job."

Dan laughed heartily, saying, "Oh, I don't know. It was great fun knocking down doors and then, of course, sampling the stuff to see if it was the real thing. Some of it was quite good and my neighbor also made great bathtub gin."

"I agree. Tasted some of it myself, ah, just to see if it was poisonous, you know," he said, laughing as he glanced over at his friend. "But, getting back to the prison, I think it will not only be good therapy but you'll be working on some of the deep problems we face in restraining men in prison. Some still believe the only treatment for prisoners is of the harshest type of cruel practices. Since the inmates have no weapons, their only retaliation for cruel practices is by food strikes and, believe me, that can lead to a mess. Sometimes they have attempted to murder a guard, usually not succeeding, but they have from time to time. So, in their own way, they retaliate."

Somewhere in the house, a clock chimed as Paddy stood and reached for a cigarette in a humidor on the sink.

"I have a program that I worked out over there which could do well in this prison." Dan fished into his pocket and pulled out a paper. "This is one of my ideas. I need to get the public interested or it won't succeed. So, I could use your help in introducing me to some movers and shakers here in the city." Shoving the paper across the table, Dan took a sip then placed the glass in the sink.

Paddy was reading the paper as he continued speaking, nodding in agreement, saying, "Boxing is it? Strangely, I still recall how amazing it was when those prisoners began playing football with their guards and a type of camaraderie took over in that prison."

"Well, you forget those prisoners were honorable men caught up in their own righteous cause, to their way of thinking. These men you speak of over here are convicted criminals and will have to be handled differently."

"Aye, that's true."

Dan's thoughts were far away, seeing those men who went on hunger strikes while imprisoned. *"It's called battle fatigue, Danny," Seamus had once explained. "Saw it in the big war when men, so weary of battle, actually threw themselves before the cannon. It can happen within prisons as well, where they'll go on a hunger strike to hasten their deaths."*

9

Placing the glass in the sink, Paddy reached for his cap and squashing the cigarette in an ashtray, said, "Well enough of that. I'll walk you to the ferry."

They strolled along the hilly streets frosted with colorful Victorian Painted Ladies who, despite the peeling face paint, ravaged by salty air and arthritic, still bore a disdainful aura as they leaned into the wind.

At Fisherman's Wharf, the two men stood quietly observing all the frantic activity on the bay with small boats arriving, dragging huge nets filled with squirming fish from the ocean as men shouted across the water, proudly advertising their catches while vying for docking space. The sharp aroma of boiling crab pots lined in rows along the sidewalks next to restaurants steamed the air and aroused hunger pangs.

"Like the ports at home, right?" Paddy nudged Dan as they dodged the spray from the hoses of men washing crab pots, and walked along the pier, passing a line of shivering tourists waiting outside a chowder house.

"Well, the prison's over there, buried in fog now," Paddy said, pointing to the north. "But its location, Danny, will remind you a little of the old country."

Dan looked away, not wanting his friend to see the loneliness in his eyes as they shook hands and he strode across the pier to board the ferry. A crowd was just emerging, spreading across the planks of the pier and hastily intermingling with the boarding passengers, while city streetcars waited along the wharf, clanging noisy greetings fusing with the shouts from the new arrivals searching for jitneys and taxis.

It was spring, a time when the fog holds its breath, creating long days of chalky light when Dan first saw the gray outline of the prison from the ferry that rocked across the bay like a kite pushed and tugged by currents of wind and water. Clad in an ill-fitting suit, he leaned elbows on the splintered railing watching the shoreline disappear beneath the fog's invisible curtain.

Running a hand along the edge of the starched white collar, memories played across his mind like a phonograph needle scratching the rusty edges of time. Spinning reminders of the past whirled in harmony with a bleating foghorn on the bay. From a vest pocket, he drew a yellowed snapshot of two young people, a grinning Dan, checkered cap balanced precariously on his head, had one arm slung carelessly across the shoulders of a friend. Carefree youth smiled back at the camera and exuberant life jingled in his pockets like loose change. Studying the picture and remembering the day they had posed in laughter on a visit to Dublin, he once more was reminded that his boyhood friend had succumbed to the effects of starvation while imprisoned. The image of that rat-infested prison with its squalor and misery would be forever etched in his memory along with the faces of those men who preferred death over imprisonment.

A large pot-bellied stove squatted on wide flat haunches in the center of the glass-enclosed lounge, crackling and spitting sparks. Long glossy wood benches with high curved backs marched in orderly rows across the deck as Dan walked toward the stove, which, after swallowing flames, burped blasts of hot air, warming his outstretched hands. Stairs led topside to the wheelhouse and below to the lower deck that housed cars in rows of shiny steel like eager horses at a racetrack gate, engines now silenced.

"S'cuse me." The voice startled Dan who glanced around at a short, portly man clad in a brown-checkered suit with striped shirt and flowery tie. An oatmeal-tinted bowler was perched on a shock of white hair clutching a ferry ticket in its plaid band. "Mind if I join you?"

Without waiting for a reply, the man plopped on the bench beside Dan, sighing deeply, and, waving a pudgy fist in the direction of the bay, said, "Can't see a thing out there now but just wait till later and it'll be a sight worth the bumpy ride and the nickel. You can see the mighty Pacific Ocean sometimes and it's so close you can smell its salty breath!"

Dan watched his new companion place a scarred briefcase on the floor and, squeezing it between scuffed black patent-leather shoes, shouted over the roar of the engines, "Yep." His

11

round face creased into a wide grin above his collar. "It's going to be a nice day once the fog lifts her skirts," his laughter was accompanied by slapping his knees hard with pudgy hands. Then, turning to Dan, he asked, "Where you headed?"

"Over there."

The prison spires were now escaping through a thick wall of fog as the men stared across the water.

"I go over twice a week," he said, yanking all the while on his tie in a vain attempt to straighten the twisted shirt collar. As the aroma of freshly-brewed coffee filled the lounge, the few remaining passengers walked across the deck to the café, leaving Dan and Angel alone.

"You're a new bull, huh?"

"I guess you mean a new guard. Yeah, but it's only a temporary job." Dan wasn't sure if his appointment was a subject for discussion yet. Paddy had not indicated that Dan's position was special and that Dan would be agitating for the innovation of a sports program against a ruling group in the prison system that had been openly vocal in their opposition.

"Well, let me introduce myself because I have a feeling we'll be seeing more of each other. I'm Herbert Angel, barrister, esquire and all," he said, extending his hand as Dan clasped it in a warm greeting and responded, "Dan Grady, recent import from Ireland. I'm pleased to meet you."

Angel slapped his fat knee and laughed, saying, "You Irish! I never understood you. No offense meant but it seems that you migrate to law enforcement when you hit this country yet in your own country, you defy the laws."

"You're so right and I can't argue with that statement." Dan smiled slightly. "However, the laws we defy aren't our own but ones foisted upon us by another country."

"Oh, oh, looks like I got off on the wrong foot and I don't want that. I do like the idea of young blood in prison work, more compassionate."

Letting a few minutes pass without a word, Herbert abruptly changed the subject. "Now, there," pointing his cigar toward the approaching shoreline. "That's the Big House. You know, the beginning of this prison was in the old hull of an abandoned ship anchored offshore."

Dan's attention was drawn to the shadowy image of a stone fortress, spires looming through the misty morning like a page from a Shakespeare tale.

"Yep, all the prisoners, men, women and children were herded aboard at night and during the daylight hours, toiled on shore building their own damned prison. They even made their own bricks for the cellblocks and walls by digging out those hills, shaping the wet mud into blocks, adding straw and drying them in the sun."

"What happened to them when the prison was finished?"

"Ah, hell, I don't know. Probably went to live inside, I guess. Why?"

At the mention of the prisoners, Dan's mind had drifted to a recurring dream about that old fortress in Dublin where many friends had been incarcerated during the Uprisings. *In the dream, the prison was abandoned and he was frantically searching the empty cells when a wizened old man, hobbling on crutches, appeared, pointing a bony finger, saying, "Where was ye? Chained to a barge and sunk, them sodgers was, lad," he said, shaking his head and spitting long streams of black tobacco juice. "Towed way out to sea they was, beyond Hy-Brasail. Them bloody English cowards did that. If ye have half a brain and a tuppence, ye'd leave this sad land."*

As the ferry creaked through the fog, people began stirring while from the lower deck the muffled roar of engines filled the morning air. The small ferry jerked, then with a loud thrashing and gnashing of gears, was slowly guided into the pier through a narrow berth as men ran and tossed ropes to others on shore, securing it to the wharf as Dan and Angel watched from the deck above.

"Well, here we are. How're you getting around? You know the prison's a piece from here."

"Walking, I guess."

"No, you're not. I've got my car below and I could use the company. Besides, it won't hurt your image none if that's what

13

you're thinking." Angel was shouting over the noise as he started down the stairs. "The officials welcome my visits as much as my clients because I bring cigars and newspapers. It makes this briefcase mighty heavy at times."

The little coupe bumped along the dirt road, lunging at all the potholes with a vengeance, bouncing and skipping through green hills alive with orange-scented wildflowers. Breezes off the bay wafted warm over old barns, farmyards with grazing cattle and an occasional farmhouse. Splintered and peeling from daily assaults of wind, sun and salt spray, the houses peered through the branches of enormous oak trees.

"Married?" Angel shouted above the rattling engine, squealing tires and crunching gravel.

"I was."

"Marriage isn't for everyone for sure and that includes me. Anyway the characters I associate with aren't fit to be around a woman."

Angel chattered on as they drove along the pockmarked road, words somersaulting over his tongue and tripping over one another in eager flight. "Just as has been the case for centuries, prisons are places where beatings with rubber hoses and lime-filled dungeons are daily occurrences. Wardens and board members are all political appointments so what the hell do they know about the care and feeding of thousands of criminals?"

While speaking with reddened face, his whole demeanor became more intense. Gripping the steering wheel tighter, pressing on the gas pedal harder and chewing the cigar stub into a smashed wad of wet tobacco, sent a message that this intense man was a true prisoners' advocate and a good person to know, Dan decided.

"You know," he said, shifting in the seat and looking slyly over at Dan, "when a man's appointed as curator of a museum or manages a zoo, they have to be qualified either as an artist of sorts or doctor of veterinary medicine. To my knowledge, not one man running this place has a solid background in prison work. Maybe some of the guards have had experience in other prisons but nothing that says they are qualified to manage a prison."

Pausing while surveying the scenery, Angel grinned, then looked over at Dan and said, "Anyway, this is the nether world; a place where heaven's forgotten; fifty-seven men are languishing on death row, one hundred women incubating in limbo and three thousand men residing a few feet from the screen door into hell. Welcome to your new world." Angel then saluted a surprised Dan.

Seeing Dan's anxious face, he laughed, saying, "Look at it this way. The men on death row are not your concern and the women have their matrons. So, all you have to deal with is what the hell to do with three thousand men caged inside a few acres. Could be worse, you know."

"How?"

"You could be unemployed."

The sun-washed village clinging to a rocky embankment over the bay seemed pickled in brine and marinated in salty sea spray. Dilapidated houses, having shed their coats of paint years ago, hung naked over the rock-bound cliffs in drunken fashion, shivering over pilings of weathered and bird-stained wood. Board sidewalks, splintered from years of wear, were strung through the village like riggings from a fisherman's dory, weaving a path from the bay to the enormous iron gates.

"At one time this place was considered a veritable fortress and escape nearly impossible. But a few years back a prisoner jumped into the bay and so far there's been no trace of him."

"Got away, huh?"

"I don't think so. Bay's full of man-eating sharks so the search was limited to watching for body parts washing ashore over the next few weeks."

Leaning across the seat, Angel grabbed the briefcase and closing the door, nodded toward the prison, saying, "Well this is it, Charley, your new home."

The broad iron gates were black links set into an adobe-colored stone fence that stretched across the width of the road with one tower by the water standing guard over the entrance. Glancing toward the tower, Dan saw a lanky guard standing by windows encircling a small room at the top, watching their

15

approach through binoculars. Angel waved casually but the man abruptly turned away, ignoring the greeting.

"That's Hanging Harry, doubles as executioner when needed. Some visitors spit at him when they walk by and he'll pretend to aim that machine gun at them. Just a little game they play. Gets extra pay for his death job. Guess you already know that all executions are by rope. And yep, they do walk those thirteen steps; twelve dedicated to the jurors and one to the judge who sent them there."

As the watch tower guard suddenly returned his stare with unfriendly eyes, Dan saw a glint from the sun's rays on the weapon peering over the half-glass window.

"Well, if it ain't the angel of mercy coming here to bestow his blessings on friends and foe." The cheery voice welcoming Angel came from the guard house by the gate.

"How're you doing Charley?" Angel thrust his hand forward, greeting the guard who now walked over and clutched the latches of the iron gates, allowing Angel to pass through.

"He calls everyone Charley." The guard was grinning as he spoke. "Guess it's easier that way. You here to sign up?" When Dan nodded, the friendly guard motioned to a chair inside the post. "Take a seat. I have to call you in."

Ignoring the chance to sit, Dan remained standing by the gates which abutted stone turrets garnished with small guard houses mounted on the peaks.

As he stared at the grim structure, a shiver raced along his spine. Soon, another guard approached and signaled to Dan who followed along the sidewalk which skirted the bay now shimmering in the late morning light.

Somewhere within the prison walls a whistle blew and the convicts who were lined along a fence smoking and watching Dan's approach with hooded eyes, disappeared. Dan soon followed them into the bowels of the prison, stepping through several heavy inner gates, discarding his familiar world as one reluctantly discards an old moth-eaten coat, yet always has fond memories of its warmth.

Chapter II

July 1926

"An eye for an eye, you damned sons-a-whores," the guard was shouting from his post high on a stone wall overlooking the dusty prison yard. A milling throng of several hundred men gathered in the exercise yard, glared in his direction, fists raised in the hot air while swirling dust eclipsed the sunlight, leaving shadows and light skipping across the yard. It was early afternoon, smoke from cigarettes held by idle hands was swirling and mixing with the dust raised by tramping feet as the prisoners congregated under the corrugated roof that tented the big yard. A few fights had erupted earlier in the day over news through the grapevine of the flogging death of a young fish a few months before and sent some to solitary confinement.

"Walrus! Ain't you the big man with a gun, huh? Stop hiding a'hind it and come on down. We ain't going to hurt you! Are you afraid of us?" The inmate was straining his neck as he observed the guard pacing along the catwalk above.

The paunchy guard with lacquered goatee and bushy sideburns, wiping sweat from his face with a red bandana, lifted the barrel of a rifle and pointing it down at the throng, slowly backed toward his post on the stone parapet containing a chair, small desk and telephone.

"Hey, big okie!" The inmate raised a clenched fist. "You're the son of a whore and fuckin' dog! Come on down, you yellow coyote!"

The fuming man, craning his neck, leaned over the parapet and glared at the restless crowd below. "What damned bastard called me a foul name? You hyenas can't get away from your pack, can you? Is there safety in numbers?"

With fists so damp with sweat clinging to the barrel of the gun like a second skin, the guard began slowly backing away from the railing.

The air was now electrified, sizzling like high tension wires on a storm-static night, as both guard and inmate measured one another. Each was cockeyed certain that death stalking the yard this afternoon, would visit the prison as surely as the dinner bell would ring at five o'clock.

Raucous laughter drowned the man's curses as the prisoners began chanting and clapping hands in a strange and eerie applause. The ground was trembling when the frantic guard turned his back on the prisoners and reached out for the telephone.

Holding the instrument high in the air and sending the roar from the yard across the wires, Walrus swung around and, in freezing disbelief, stared into a pair of steely green-flecked eyes. Grasping a crude stiletto, cleverly honed from a screwdriver, the prisoner leered into the face of fright. An incoherent curse, strangling in blood pouring from the viciously sliced throat, teetered in the sea of red sprayed across the walls of the guardhouse as well as dripping along the parapet. As quickly as he came, the assailant clambered down a rope attached to the railing and disappeared.

"It's done," reverberated across the compound as the men fled through doors and clanking gates, vanishing within the enormous belly of the prison. A few inmates remained, nonchalantly raking the yard and never glancing away from their work.

The alarm blasted across the prison grounds as the chanting continued alerting all of the men sleeping in the dormitory.

Asleep in the barracks above the narrow building that crept along the water's edge, Dan Grady was jarred awake by the shrieking alarm. Quickly joining other cursing men, he jumped from the bed, pulling on pants while stumbling through doors toward the armory. The armory, a tall building resembling a lighthouse, guarded the main entrance to the prison and was protected by a draw bridge across a large concrete culvert similar to a castle moat of ancient times.

Trotting through the inner yard, passing cellblocks where inmates were being hastily herded and counted, Dan heard clanking doors echoing over the obscenities of irate guards.

"What the hell?" The shouted curse hung in the still air as the group of guards stopped and stared in disbelief at the quiet yard where a handful of convicts were busily raking leaves, ignoring the presence of the men.

With a southern drawl as thick as maple syrup coating his tongue, the guard, Southpaw, who had signed-up with Dan, turned toward him with questioning eyes.

"Well, doesn't this put those damned long hours of indoctrination all to hell? Hey, we got warned about these creeps, you know; how they'd stick a knife in ya as easily as look atcha, but not this. We were never told they behaved so nicely, huh? We were told they were real bad boys! Look at 'em! Like little boy scouts over there, raking leaves! I don't like the fucking damn atmosphere in here!"

Looking around, Dan noticed red paint dripping down the wall into the dusty weeds decorating the base of the north wall and, upon closer inspection, realized that it was blood streaming from the broken body sprawled above, legs flung apart, head twisted in a grotesque position. A crudely-shaped knife was seen gleaming in the sun, resting beside a human ear, deafened forever. For the guards, this was the first clue that a gruesome murder had been the cause of the uproar.

"Get the knife over to the front office!" A white-coated man bending over the inert body on the parapet was angrily shouting orders from above.

Crossing the yard with the evidence of mayhem, murder and vengeance, Dan headed for the front office where an officer took the bloody weapon, rope and, staring in shock at the ear, gingerly accepted it from Dan. "I'll take care of this, uh," he said, shuddering. "You men can turn in your weapons now," nodding toward the armory and turning away.

19

Accompanied by Southpaw, Dan was still puzzling over the murder and the shorn ear.

"What the hell can a man do?" Southpaw grumbled. "The cons outnumber us and the only protection we got is this stupid billy-club. We're not allowed any weapons inside unless there's a riot."

"Hell,! That guard had a loaded weapon and it didn't help him. I'm just wondering why they didn't take his gun," Dan said with a puzzled look.

"Probably didn't have time. Where would they hide it?"

"That's possible but in the short time we've been here, I know these men are capable of performing Houdini stunts that even the great man himself couldn't have done. So, dismantling and concealing a rifle wouldn't be a problem. Maybe they're just thumbing their noses at us!"

"Think we're stupid 'cause we're new on the job, I guess." Southpaw was assigned to the midnight watch on the north wall with Dan. Passing one another along the parapet in the solitary darkness had given them some moments to share a cigarette and become acquainted.

Southpaw who came from the southern part of Alabama where thick brushy undergrowth near the swamps and rivers concealed alligators twelve-feet and longer, said,

"I ain't as afeared of them critters as I am of these here critters," he laughed one night as they shared a smoke on the parapet. "Leastways, the gators jest take one bite and you're gone, no suffering. These cons, hey, you just don't know where, how or when their bite'll strike 'cause they like to watch us squirm."

Dan joined in laughter with the burly southerner whose size of over six-feet belied his soft nature.

The bay was tossing its white mane angrily the following evening as Dan strode along the parapet overlooking the prison yard. Wind whipped across the waters stinging his face with salty spray and soaking his mackintosh. Watching small fishing vessels flee into a nearby harbor, he stepped around blood stains from the guard's murder that not even the wild storm could wipe away, and puzzled over the crime.

"He was marked for death," an officer had explained to the neophytes later that morning. "The only problem is, we don't know why."

Dan lit a Camel with his silver cigarette lighter, puffing vigorously while cupping his hands to shield it from the wind, and wondered above all why he was here.

Witts End, A Tavern

The bay was breathless this evening, the color of old pewter. An approaching storm that had been waiting in the wings for several hours, soon bellowed across the hills, shuddering the earth and spitting long strings of light across the gray skies. Large puffy clouds like newly-shorn, lanolin-laced wool were stacked-up along the horizon and the drums of thunder reverberated in the amphitheater of the mountains. In the hollow of its armpit, the bay gave shelter to a few fleeing boats that anchored in a small cove near the prison. The guard in the tower watched with anxious eye as the boats arrived too close to his world.

Witt's End, a salty old tavern, was situated at the far end of the village, basking like a beached seal on a rocky ledge over the waters of the bay and was a welcome retreat for the guards coming off twelve-hour shifts. With the nearest town several miles away and transportation limited to a small bus arriving and departing twice a day, most of the employees of the prison and village residents spent their leisure time in the little café.

On this blustery evening, Dan strode through the swinging doors, across a planked floor carpeted in sawdust, toward a round table cramped beneath a water-streaked window.

He was *howdied* by the bartender, Louie Wittener, whose clever name for the tavern was credited to his wife, as he related the story to Dan one day. "When we were remodeling it, she hollered about a name for the place and I said I don't know, I'm at my wit's end and she shouted that's it! Witt's End! Pretty neat, huh? 'Course if you don't know our name, it means nothing."

Today Louie was intent upon pouring some home brew into frosty mugs and sliding a foaming one along the glossy mahogany bar toward Dan. Louie's home brew was the popular drink in town despite prohibition, which was ignored by most of the village.

Across the room seated at a table hugging the wall, Ham Crane, a silver-haired man engrossed in a game of checkers with a worn-looking man sprouting a goatee, leaned on an ivory-handled cane and peered over rimless glasses at the men. "This tavern is the only beacon of light in this damned community of lost souls! Anyone sending for the sheriff will have to deal with me," he shouted, waving his cane in the air.

Dan joined in the laughter as Louie approached the table with a grease-stained menu tucked under one arm. A large apron rode below his beltline, losing its daily struggle with the corpulent belly.

"The sheriff? Hell, he was just here the other night for his dinner."

"Is that so?" Ham Crane said, with raised frosty eyebrows. "And what did he eat, crow?"

Laughter filled the room, spilling out along the water's edge while everyone shared in a special camaraderie, knowing the folks in town considered them outcasts to be shunned as quickly, if not quicker than the inmates.

"You mean after he gave that speech at the town meeting about policing all those places breaking the law? And when someone asked about my place, he swore he never came out here 'cause the prison employees' police their own town."

"Ain't that the truth!" Catfish, a guard seated at the bar with one fist wrapped around a frosty mug of beer said as he scratched his head. "Hey! He called this place a town?"

This remark brought another round of laughter. Catfish, a genial man with thinning hair and lanky body, was a favorite of the prisoners who knew only too well that his time-off was spent fishing the waters of the bay with little or almost no luck. He loved to talk and the inmates were his audience, actually a captive audience. Consequently, in their eyes, Catfish seemed an appropriate handle for this guard.

Turning back to Dan, Louie wiped his forehead with the apron. "Chowder's good today; oysters right from the bay here," he said, gesturing toward the churning waters.

"Okay. Bowl of chowder sounds good." Dan glanced around the room in the casual way one does when in familiar surroundings. A few customers were scattered around and, with the exception of Ham Crane, his checkerboard companion and Catfish, Dan didn't recognize anyone from the prison. The aroma emanating from the kitchen was blanketing the room as Dan settled into the warm cocoon of home-cooking and new friends.

Ham Crane glanced up from the checkerboard, asking, "How's the investigation going?"

"Are you asking me?"

"Yep."

Dan was puzzled at the knowledge this man had of the activities within the prison walls. Most of the cottages in the little village housed prison employees with some scattered fishermen and a few old timers, among whom Ham Crane was numbered. After spending his day at Witt's End playing checkers and eating two meals, Ham retreated to a solitary room in the widow Abbott's rooming house, a shabby two-storied structure clinging tenaciously to a grassy hillside overlooking the bay and the prison gates.

"Mostly considered by everyone as one of our eccentric treasures," was the usual response by any resident when questioned about Ham Crane. A waiflike man with shocking white hair and neatly trimmed mustache, Ham walked with a cane, exuding personal charm without sending a clue about his personal life. Who was he? How did he end-up living in this remote village so close to a prison and so far from a town? Could he be the mysterious con-boss Dan had heard about? He was an intriguing character and, to Dan, an interesting enigma.

"Aw shit, I tried," Angel had once responded to Dan's question. "No one knows where he came from or why he's here. According to the old timers, he's always been here like maybe he was left over from that original abandoned ship. He's old enough, or, at least, looks it."

23

"What investigation?" Dan peered across the room, wondering how much Crane knew about the guard's murder. The local papers had carried it in small print on the last page behind the obituaries.

"I think you know that I mean the murder of Walrus on the north wall."

"Ah yes, him." Louie joined in the conversation, jerking a thumb toward the prison. "That old Walrus wasn't one of my favorite customers and not liked at the prison."

The stillness in the room was pierced by a woman's shrill voice escaping through the kitchen doors, yelling, "You don't know that, Louie."

"She can hear the bloody algae growing out there, that woman." Louie waved a fist as he walked around the long bar and began loudly scrubbing beer steins in the small sink.

Finishing the meal, Dan started toward the door when Ham Crane called, "Hey, Dan. You know that guard was always in trouble."

Long slender fingers, yellowed with tobacco stains and tipped with polished pearl-coated nails moved restlessly as he drew a tapered cigarette from its bed in a silver case and lighting it as he spoke. Sensing that Ham had more to say, Dan slid a chair over to the table while Ham's companion let out an audible sigh.

Staring at Dan, Ham frowned, pausing as if reflecting on his next words, then looked across the bay and back at the checker board before saying, "I once worked here and, unfortunately, I know his kind. He came from the south, Georgia, I believe, and worked in a prison there. As I recall, he was a firm adherent of the chain-gang method of controlling men. Even wanted to use that system on the quarry here but I stopped it, yes indeed!"

While speaking, he continued intently studying the red and black checkerboard squares and continued, "You probably have heard that at one time, men were placed in deep holes while sacks of lime were dropped down to destroy their lungs. Not anymore, of course. That went out with the floggings, or so I'm told. Well, he was an active participant in doling out those terrible punishments. Always had his hand raised when volunteers were recruited for punishments. A true sadist, if you ask me. In fact, I heard that he had beaten a fish with a rubber hose recently, supposedly to thwart the kid's plans to escape. Later, the kid died."

"So, do you think his murder was revenge for past cruel punishments?"

"Oh, I'm sure of it, sir. You'll soon learn that the prisons in this country are like a chain of auto courts, in a way. Criminals travel around in similar groups, know one another, and are aware of each prison's treatment of the men. It's possible that one or more cons in the crowd that day had been deliberately sent to the prison for that single purpose."

"That's an interesting thought. Never realized these inmates were so organized. And, you say, they travel around the country? In groups, bumping into each other?"

"Well, I meant that theory is possible, considering the years these men have been incarcerated in other prisons, as well."

"You know, I've heard rumors about a prison boss who is suspected of making life and death decisions regarding both prisoners and guards. Know anything about him or even if the rumor is true?" Dan asked.

Ham Crane sniffed, turning worried eyes on his inquisitor and said, "I have no knowledge of this at all, sir."

"Tell me about the Hole and the dungeons. I need to know what these men have been through before I can help them."

Looking up from the board, Ham's eyes narrowed as he said, "Are you serious? You want to help them? Sir, you're here to control them and that's all!"

"Admittedly I've only been here a short time. Don't see much on night patrol but I'm aware of complaints from the guards about some medieval methods of punishment."

Watching a smirk surf across Ham's lips, Dan was aware of the man's contemptuous feelings not only for him but for the prisoners as well and said, "Anyway, I think I have a solution to some of the problems."

"You have a magic solution?" Ham asked, face twisted into a wry expression as he studied Dan who replied, "Athletics."

Ham laughed as he leaned back in the chair, saying, "Ah, you have plans for a country club complete with tennis courts and swimming pools! Believe you're not the first to propose such a ridiculous scheme."

"No. But locking them away all weekend only breeds more violent behavior. With sports, they would at least be occupied."

"Don't you realize you're dealing with criminals not school boys in a dorm?"

"I learned that during my first week here, sir."

Chapter III

October 1926

The fog-wrapped weeks teetered into months as Dan continued pacing the north wall. Since the murder of the guard, the prisoners had settled into an uneasy truce with their jailers.

"Got a light?" A gravelly voice echoed along the stone walls as Dan looked around from his post to see a crooked smile surrounded by candid blue eyes under shaggy white eyebrows. Reaching into his pocket for a match and lighting the proffered cigarette, Dan studied the duty guard who was sharing his watch.

"Thanks." Exhaled smoke rode herd on each word as he gestured toward the cellblocks below, saying, "Supposed to be a full moon tonight but I don't hear any noise from down there and I don't like it, too quiet."

"Yeah, I know the moon usually drives 'em crazy, banging on cell bars with their tin plates. It's like feeding time at the zoo."

"I'd sure as hell rather be there tonight," and while stretching out his hand to shake Dan's hand, he spoke in a voice that strung words together in a quivering drawl. "Sawyer Buck also known as Sawbucks to our gentlemen boarders here. Heard you were on my duty watch tonight and I've been wanting to meet you."

"Why?"

"Oh, you should know by now that every word uttered here is tossed around the prison like rice at a wedding. Just heard about some of your ideas, that's all."

"The athletic program, you mean?"

"Sounded good to me but to make any changes in this place would take another hundred years. It would take half that to even reach the ears of the governor."

"Well, I have to start sometime."

Raising a foot, Sawbucks rested it on the low railing of the fence and with an elbow on his raised knee, leaned into the wind. "There are some guards here who might make life hell for you."

"Why?"

"Aw, you know, some of these guys are real mean; hate the cons and are here 'cause they can't find work any place these days that pays this well. Anyway, they say that sports would be coddling the men. They'd be coddled yeggs!" His laughter echoed and skipped across the empty yards, bouncing off the buildings.

"Yeggs, coddled yeggs, get it?" Looking at Dan's impassive face, Sawbucks continued chuckling. "Sorry about that pun. Couldn't resist it, you know."

Dan, ignoring the humor, replied, "Well, it's no surprise that some guards will think sports is coddling."

"Yeah, but then there are others like Tom "Roller" Skates and Wally "Pepper" Salte who are the salt of the earth, no pun intended this time." Laughing at something remembered, he flipped the cigarette butt into a large receptacle filled with sand. "Yeah, these cons, soon as they learn about a ridiculous habit or a name they can make sound like puke, we're stuck with it for life."

"Maybe a sense of humor is needed to survive in here."

"You got that right."

"Say, what about that old man who hangs out at the diner all the time? He seems to know a lot about the workings inside here."

"Oh, you mean Ham Crane? Sharp mind for an old guy, must be close to ninety. Claims to have been a warden here once but there's no record of that. Course, the records in the old days were haphazardly kept. Strange guy, though."

"Could he be a prison boss?" Dan frowned.

"Hey, you'll hear all kinds of rumors in this mill, believe me. Half are not true and the other half are lies."

After leaving Sawbucks, Dan walked back toward his post as a feeling of apprehension crept along his spine. In one corner of the heavens, the Big Dipper spilled over a pitcher of milky stars illuminating a portion of the sky. Strange sounds shaped the night, creating an eerie atmosphere. Just as he stepped from his post to patrol the other end of the wall, an echo skipped across the silent yard like a dream loosened from earthly bonds, palpitating in the uneasy quiet of the prison. Peering over the wall, Dan saw the shadow of a man crossing the yard.

"Who goes?" Dan pointed his rifle in that direction.

"He's okay-a trustee." A voice from the nearby post carried across the parapet.

The guard was leaning against the wall, hat cocked back on his head, cigarette dangling from thick lips while smoke swept around his head. Lowering the gun, Dan walked over toward the man, who upon stubbing the cigarette under foot, lit another and smiled, saying, "Odd duck. Always thought he was in the wrong institution-should be in a nut house." A hoarse laugh revealed deep dimples engraved in a weather-beaten face. Squinting, he reached out a hand in greeting and introduced himself, saying, "Wally Salte. The cons call me Pepper. Aren't they clever?"

Laughing, Dan said, "Yeah, they're ingenious all right. Wonder what tag I'll get."

"Aw, probably have licensed you already."

Nodding, Dan was still scanning the yard and feeling uneasy.

"Yeah," Pepper said gesturing toward the yard below as if reading Dan's mind. "He's kitchen help, Riley something or other. Never can remember names or numbers! Cleans till midnight then walks back to his cellblock. You can set your watch by him. Speaking of time, thought you was off tonight."

"I'm working two shifts tonight. Won't be off till morning." Dan paused and frowned, saying, "Say, if he works until midnight what's he doing out in the yard now? It's only eleven" he said, peering at the watch he pulled from his vest pocket.

"Don't know. Maybe he's sick, or something." Pepper's voice trailed off as he studied the prison yard. "Well," turning around and reaching into the post, he brought out a thermos. "Want a swig?"

"No thanks. I've got to get back to my post."

"Nice meeting you." As Pepper poured coffee into a metal cup, the rising steam mingled with the strong aroma of whiskey. Walking back along the wall, Dan wondered about some guards walking walls on night shifts who brought whiskey to pass the long hours and keep off the chills although it was definitely breaking the rules.

"Makes a guy sleepy, not alert if there's a problem in there," Sawbucks had once remarked. "Some have been seen dozing in their guardhouse. I haven't seen it and if I do, sure, I'll report him if that does any good."

Tonight, Dan also wondered about Pepper's apparent dismissal of a prisoner in the yard at the wrong time. And didn't he see a signal between the two men just briefly as he turned away? He wasn't sure because at that moment, a bright searchlight beam swooped across the yard, slightly blinding him.

The following morning, Dan was summoned to the warden's office by Jake Newton, who was acting warden in Rogers' absence. Maybe the meeting wouldn't last too long, he mused walking across the lawn, because he had just walked off a second shift on the wall and was desperate for sleep.

From the moment they had met during his initial indoctrination, Dan liked this red-haired, pug-nosed man whose sense of humor alleviated the stressful prison work. "Once you walk through those doors out there," Jake had pointed to the front gate on that day, saying, "and enter the corridors of these cellblocks, you become like them, your prisoners. You learn to swivel, dodge and jump at the slightest sound. Always on the alert, you no longer are part of that casual crowd over there in the city whose only concern is the latest ballpark score because you have begun to think like these guys," he said, pointing to the cages down the hallway. "You know how a boxer in the ring shuffles around, flat-footed, swinging and punching at the air? All the time, he's enclosed in this ring, yet he ignores that." Jake began two-stepping around the room, punching at an invisible adversary while demonstrating the boxing technique. "But all the time his eye is on that circling opponent, waiting for the right moment and then pow! An easy k.o.! An easy death! Well, the boxer, that's him over there in the cellblock," pointing to the cells, "and the opponent, that's you over here, circling him, cagily watching but no eye contact and the referee, well, he's the state of California, keeping his eye glued on you."

This morning, Jake leaned back in his chair while pointing to another chair and said, "Sit, Dan, sit. While the warden's away, I have to perform all the odious duties that he usually manages to avoid even when he's here, but the worst is the gallows and all who go there."

He was shuffling a stack of papers, inking some with a red stamp and shoving others into a wastebasket teetering by his feet. "Damned thing is that I need some help here so I decided that it was time you assisted me in officiating at this one." Seeing Dan's surprised face, he leaned back in the swivel chair, crossing arms behind his head and looked across the garden toward the blue waters beyond.

"When I heard the rumors about your desire to bring sports to the restless savages in this jungle, I have to admit I was really shocked. You want cons playing baseball? Give me a break! Then, the more I thought about it, the more it began to make a hell of a lot of sense! Our biggest problem here besides overcrowding and rotten food, is behavior. Every week, men are sent to solitary confinement for only minor infractions because we don't know what the hell to do with them. They aren't that bad, they're just pushed into one another and after a while, it wears on frayed nerves and all that shit." Pausing for a few moments and, swiveling around in the chair, he added, "I was raised in Chicago where we had to use our fists to survive. But I never used them

31

except to defend myself and would never use these big hams against anyone weaker. So, anyway, welcome aboard."

Watching Dan lighting a Camel, Jake smiled, then continued, saying, "I usually never read the charges but since you're going to be at the execution, I'll tell you a little about this guy. Sometimes it helps to be reminded of the crime when forced to watch this procedure."

Sighing, he picked up some papers and read: "He started along the crime trail at a young age by torturing and beheading animals on his family farm. Later, his parents, impressed by his paintings of the beheaded animals, sent him to a private art school where his favorite subject was sketching nude women. Eventually these nudes were prostitutes. Being a self-proclaimed Picasso, he liked to paint the torso with some of the victim's blood minus the head. There has been no final count on the number of murdered women or where they are buried. Even he forgot where he disposed of these mutilated bodies."

In the quiet room, neither man spoke for long minutes while Dan, looking through the sun-soaked windows that framed the bay, lit another cigarette while blowing smoke heavily through his nostrils and asked, "Did he confess?"

"Oh hell, yes," Jake snorted. "Not only confessed but bragged about losing count." Commenting as he rose from the chair and walked toward the door, "The reports I've been receiving are fairly positive that this might be one of the last hangings in this prison."

"Is that so? What's going in its place?"

"I heard it's the gas chamber. I might add the warden disagrees with those who think there's more suffering in hanging than with gas. Says the gas chamber execution will last longer and consequently be harder on the witnesses. Hey, don't look surprised. Witnesses are hard to find! There's an interesting story with this, Dan. A few years ago, before my time, the rope snapped-off the head of a man and, Jesus Christ, it rolled across into the spectator section, open eyes, blood spurting on some of the witnesses and splattering the walls like shit hitting a ceiling fan, and fuming guards racing to retrieve it while a spectator fainted."

"What happened?"

"No one knows but that was the beginning of a search for a more humane approach to execution, at least a more humane one for the spectators. You know, by law, we need them."

In the silence, both men were caught up in the imagery of that hanging. Jake sighed and looked across the room at the splashing bay. "Now, shall we go over the procedure before you head in there tomorrow? No pun intended!" His laughter filled the room as he reached across the desk for a file folder.

The barracks room was almost empty when Dan arrived after his shower and climbed into bed. Dark curtains placed to filter out the daylight could not filter out the grim thoughts of the following day.

The building housing the gallows was slung low along the water's edge with one wall defiantly staring at the front gates, visible to any casual observer. The sixty-foot room held a large scaffold that stood ominously, casting shadows along the walls like a grotesque actor waiting for the footlights to go on in the gray room. Thirteen steps led to the platform that created the illusion of a stage for the actor waiting for rehearsals to commence.

The room reeked with the musty stale breath of a morgue and the air was shrouded with memories of dangling ropes along with the whiskey breath of the hangman. It was a place where no pulse throbbed, no voice echoed and where even the walls were blind--a windowless grotto from which death held the only exit.

The prisoner, a thin, balding man, arrived in a dazed condition, glassy-eyed and barefoot with hands tied behind his back, escorted by two guards, a chaplain, Jake and Dan. As he struggled to mount the scaffold without the aid of the guards who had stopped at the foot of the steps, he turned to study the audience, as if searching for a familiar face. All the male witnesses were seated in a row of folding chairs near the stage and nervously looked away, avoiding the frightened eyes of the lone actor. "A one-act play," a reporter later wrote, "with an actor who failed to capture his audience."

Since smoking was prohibited in this building, one witness clung tightly to a squashed cigarette butt, turning it over and over in his fingers, flakes of tobacco drifting lazily to the floor.

The practiced hands of the hangman began measuring the trembling man, a slow and tedious procedure that was essential because the exact length of the rope would bring the least pain for the man. "Otherwise he might slowly strangle," the hangman had explained earlier to the witnesses. While performing his job, Hanging Harry, who always carried a book of prayers in a back pocket, reached for the book and mumbled, "he reaps that which he sows." His voice echoed in the room, bouncing off the walls as the astonished spectators watched, mesmerized. Then a black hood was placed over the condemned man's head and he was slowly led to the rope where Harry arranged a large knot carefully and meticulously under one ear.

On a wall high above the scaffold, a large clock displayed the hour, minute and seconds on a black and white face as its hands inched unashamedly toward the hour of six.

In the grim silence, the chaplain continued murmuring incoherent prayers in a measured tone, never glancing away from the Bible he white-knuckled. Beads of perspiration skimming along his forehead and down his neck, stained the white collar. Somewhere a bell pealed, striking six notes while in the silent stone fortress thousands of men waited in their cellblocks.

When Jake raised his hand, a trapdoor was sprung open, guided by three guards hidden behind the scaffold, each holding a string, with only one releasing the trap door. The prisoner's neck broke instantly, the snap reverberating across the room as a spectator gasped but the heart beat for another ten minutes as the witnesses and a doctor with a stethoscope patiently waited.

Meanwhile the body began disposing of wastes dripping down the naked legs and joining the pants on the floor. The foul-smelling odors rose from the concrete floor, engulfing the room and floating through doors just thrown open. This odiferous validation that death had definitely arrived, joined by the tolling bell, announced the completion of the execution while along the cellblocks prisoners were released from their cells and the hive began humming again.

When the reporters rushed over to question Jake, Dan quickly exited and gripped by nausea, rushed to the barracks with churning stomach and dry heaves.

Informer, the editor of the prison newspaper, Keeper of the Mews, reported the hanging in the most sympathetic notes he had ever written.

"The law with regard to capital punishment is swift and sure, especially in the case of one who has no friends or money and who even lacks parental love. It was noted that the executed man's parents enjoyed a lavish repast in the officer's dining room while they laughed and chatted with the same men who aided in the execution of their son. After requesting second helpings of the delicious meal to be taken home, the dead prisoner's parents announced that they had decided to bury their son in Boot Hill because, if asked, he would wish to be with his friends. Of course, he was never asked."

Chapter IV

August 1929

The years hurtled by like meteors in search of a dark night as Dan moved through the ranks to the position of lieutenant and the prisoners finally settled on a name that would stick with him through life, Loot.

With his new rank, Dan was assigned a small bungalow within the prison compound and an office in an adobe building wrapped around a brick courtyard. This was surrounded on three sides by a wide veranda peppered with honeysuckle and bougainvillea vines. Rose bushes growing in profusion bordered lawns in an adjacent area christened Garden Beautiful by the inmates of an earlier time.

"This is the first place the fish will be taken for booking, fingerprinting and job assignments which will be your job," Jake said, walking Dan through the gardens and along a brick path that inmates had worn thin over the years. Since his promotion, Dan had requested Sawbucks as an aide and the office was soon tagged by the prisoners as the Five & Dime. Early in Dan's career, some inmates decided he must be a native of Finland due to his large frame, light skin and blue eyes so he was referred to as the Big Fin.

"Where the hell's Finland?" One prisoner complained to the prison newspaper and his response was a volume of mail. Some suggested that Finland was not a place but another name for finished in Latin, aka, ain't we all finished! While others suggested that it's a hot bath taken after a swim in icy water and why don't we all try it as part of an exercise program out there in the bay?

Informer noted in that week's edition that the last suggestion was the perfect answer since the Loot wants and is itching for a regular exercise program in the form of sports and isn't swimming the most all-around sport?

"Yeah," commented a guard who also wrote his opinion in the paper. "You want an all-around sport! All around the tip of the bay and out to sea, right?"

As the debate continued weekly in the prison newspaper, Dan ignored the snide references to his sports program by the guards and also by Whistler, the warden's assistant. They were against it and had loudly proclaimed their views in news items in the city newspapers: "Absolutely ridiculous! Never will these prisoners ever participate in any recreation program involving outsiders or, for that matter, even themselves. They will remain where they belong, behind bars and locked in cells on weekends."

On the day the latest edition of the paper came out, Jake commented on the uproar as he walked with Dan to the mess for lunch.

"Shit, Dan! This controversy is good for the cons and us, don't you see? It keeps their minds busy on something besides plotting escapes and the quickest way to kill us without getting caught."

"Oh hell, I knew that I'd be skating uphill when I first hit this prison and saw the need for an athletic program, so those remarks don't surprise me."

Along with Sawbucks, Dan was assigned an office staff consisting of five prisoners and his search began for men with clerical backgrounds. Unfortunately, only a few of the thousands of men were qualified to work in an office. But that didn't deter many from applying, knowing that office work was doing easy time.

"I guess this says something about the characters we have in here." Sawbucks laughed as he slid some paper into a typewriter. "We need some white collar men."

"The way things are going out there in the big world," Dan said, smiling, "they'll be arriving pretty soon."

Studying the applications one day with Sawbucks, Dan decided that since none of them qualified, he would selectively pick those with athletic backgrounds. This would be his first step toward organizing his sports program without interference from the warden's office. The first one he chose was Benny, a former professional boxer serving a life sentence for murder with a lethal weapon, his fists.

Sitting at his new desk, Dan was debating on whether to hire Benny now or wait a few months until Whistler and friends wouldn't question his motives. Looking across the gardens, he saw a wrinkled knot of trouble headed toward the office and he rushed out to intercept the reeling prisoner.

Years of dissipation swore allegiance to his face and when he smiled, a wide space with several missing teeth testified to the neglect of both body and spirit.

"I've been a heller all my life, Loot," Willie whined, a wet spray escaping through a gap in his teeth.

"Okay, Willie, come along, you're drunk." Dan snapped as he grabbed the little man by his shirt collar.

"Varnish, Loot," he said, hiccupping with each step.

"Coffin varnish you mean."

Trying to remain upright, Willie sagged against Dan and slowly crumpled to the ground.

They made a curious pair crossing the yard, the big man in uniform and the small frayed gray bundle stumbling alongside, half-walking, half-dragging his feet.

"Aw shit, Loot!" The sergeant gasped at the sight. "What the hell do I do with him?"

"Admit him to the hospital. He's seriously ill!" Dan said, dropping the man on the floor.

"Hospital! Hell! He's drunk! He needs a flogging!"

"He may need a flogging but he's not getting one as long as I'm in charge here."

"Yes sir."

Several inmates within range watched in awe as the guard yanked the unresisting man from the floor by the seat of the pants, dragging him toward the hospital, his curses mingling with Willie's hiccups.

"Well, I'll be damned," a convict stuttered over the type-writer as Dan glared in his direction.

The following day Dan was called on the carpet.

This summons came as no surprise to Dan who had expected it and, lighting a Camel, strode calmly from the office, stuffing the crumpled package of cigarettes into a coat pocket.

Bets had been placed among the office staff. Some said Dan would be canned within twenty-four hours and Willie would be flogged. Others said Dan would be merely reprimanded and Willie would be flogged anyway. Yet still others said that Dan would be figuratively flogged, like being forced to share an office with Whistler, then demoted to walking the north wall again.

The prisoners held their breath as Dan walked with deliberate step toward the administration building moored upon a knoll overlooking the compound. The convicts had found a friend, albeit a gruff, detached man but one who had for a moment exposed himself to the x-ray eyes of men adept in the art of psychoanalysis. To these men, the close quarters that breed contempt and dissention also bred students of the psyche, men with a *ouija-board* clairvoyance.

The confrontation with the upper echelon was short, explosive and an eye-opener for Dan. The oak-paneled office curtained with cigarette and cigar smoke clinging tenaciously to the walls and ceiling, was quiet as Dan entered. A uniformed man with hooded eyes was seated at an enormous walnut desk and returned Dan's look with unconcealed curiosity. Whistler, standing by the desk, his Adam's apple bobbing like a cork in the bay, averted restless eyes. The third man was Jake who stood by a sliding glass door and merely acknowledged Dan's presence with a slight nod.

As Warden Rogers rose, king-size body unfolding and blotting out the sunlight, smoke bellowed from his mouth while shaggy white hair jutted above sooty eyebrows and trailed in sideburns outlining his jaw. A rumpled khaki shirt, open at the neckline, hung loosely over his massive frame while from a wide leather belt, a revolver dangled carelessly on one hip. For long moments he studied Dan who returned the penetrating look without flinching. As the warden motioned toward a chair, Dan refused, saying, "I don't believe this is a social visit, warden," and remained standing. His response brought an immediate reaction from the chain-smoking assistant, Whistler, who, seeming to border on the ragged edge of hysteria, said, "We were discussing hiring practices and............"

"I'll handle this." With a wave of his hand, Rogers angrily dismissed the man.

Whistler, so tagged by the inmates because at one time he was always seen with a whistle hanging around his neck, sank into the chair where he crossed his legs and twitched one foot in aggravation.

Turning to Dan, Rogers spoke in a calm voice. "Jake says that he didn't give any okay for Willie to be taken to the hospital."

"That's right, he didn't."

"Well, why did you?"

"Because, sir, he was gravely ill and would have died without medical help, in my opinion."

"He was ill, my foot!" Whistler jumped from the chair saying, "Drunk, you mean."

Rogers glared at his associate as Dan realized the strange relationship between the men. It was obvious that Rogers granted Whistler a greater amount of authority, relieving himself of many burdens.

"Furniture varnish is not liquor. It's deadly."

"Nevertheless, you defied our rules." Whistler glared across the room as Dan replied. "I told Jake from the beginning that on my watch there would be no floggings and the Hole only in extreme cases or where another man's life is in danger."

Rogers, impatiently drumming his fingers on the desk, waited for Jake to speak.

"It's true that we agreed each man is to run his watch the best way he knows, which was fine with me as long as he remains within certain regulations," Jake said evenly without looking at Dan. Then, reflecting on his words, added, "And flogging is not in the regulations, as we all know."

Rogers, aware of the combustible nature of flogging which had been cited several times by the parole board as cruel punishment yet still used on occasion, did not immediately respond while he continued staring at the men. Then, glancing down at a letter on his desk, he said, "Is it true, Dan, that you broke-up a racial fight last week by stringing some rope and handing the men boxing gloves?"

"That's so." Dan started to smile at the memory.

"Where did you get the gloves?"

"I boxed a little in my day and brought some gloves with me, just in case."

"Just in case of what?"

"I'd hopefully introduce the sport into a prison."

Rogers impatiently waved his hand, saying, "That's not a subject for discussion here, sir." Glancing sternly over at Dan, he continued drumming his fingers on the desktop and asked, "Did you know those men were particularly vicious leaders of gangs here and deserved severe punishment, not sports?"

Rogers had now started shuffling the papers around on the desk as he spoke.

"Right. And after they went three rounds, they were sent to the dungeon for a week."

"I see." Rogers rubbed his whiskers with one hand while staring at Dan.

"Also," Jake hastily added, "those damned cons went like friends, talking about their boxing strategy. Never saw anything like it in my whole damned life!"

While Dan was patiently waiting for a suspension or even a dismissal, the telephone rang. Picking up the phone and listening as a screeching voice came over the wires, Rogers yelled into it, "Blow the noon whistle early! And find out what the hell's wrong!" He slammed the instrument back into its cradle and lit another cigarette with nervous hands.

As Dan also lit a cigarette, the door burst open and a guard entered, followed by a stubby convict, face peppered with freckles, pale eyes inked in fear.

"Pigeon has a message from the yard."

Swallowing hard, Pigeon stole a furtive glace over at Dan and spoke haltingly, words sticking like tar to the roof of his mouth. "They want the Loot back in his office by noon, sir, or else."

"Or else, what?" Rogers said, fuming as he stared at the prisoner.

Pigeon's eyes opened wider with fear in the presence of not only the warden but all the other officials and he stammered, "Or else another hunger strike, sir."

The stillness enveloping the room created a tension that was palpable while the men stared at Dan as if he were an apparition that would suddenly vaporize before their eyes.

"Who's running this damned prison?" Whistler's face was flushed with anger. "Let them strike! They're all too fat anyway!"

"All right, Pigeon," Rogers said. He threw a look at Whistler while Pigeon stared open-mouthed at the livid man. "Tell them we received their message."

Rogers looked over at the clock as Pigeon rushed from the room, trembling with eagerness as the bearer of such an important dispatch.

"Jesus!" Rogers collapsed into his chair, saying, "What next?"

As the warden slumped into the chair, Dan wondered if he was praying or cursing.

"What next?" Whistler stepped nimbly to the desk and reached for the telephone. "I'll tell you what's next!"

"What the hell do you think you're doing?" Rogers suddenly looked frightened.

"Ordering an immediate lockdown and we'll find the ringleaders. They're candidates for solitary confinement for a month at least!"

Jake rushed across the room and snatched the instrument from the startled man, "Like hell you will." Turning to Rogers and in a calm voice, he said, "Warden, send Dan back to his office and have it announced over all the speakers in the mess hall and yard."

Rogers glanced sharply at Dan who was wondering about a situation that had reversed in the matter of a few minutes. Studying the men in the room, Dan, to his chagrin, realized that at this moment the prisoners were in charge of the prison, gleefully intimidating the warden by throwing his office into chaos, aware of his fear that hunger strikes would damage his career and even lead to his dismissal.

"The goddamned press will be swarming all over the place by tonight," he shouted, glaring across at Dan. Then, regaining his composure, he turned to Jake, saying, "Why the hell am I taking orders from you?"

"Well, sir, it's about time you listened to other voices," he said, darting a glance at an incensed Whistler who remained standing by the desk.

"Guess there's no question about who's running this place." Sarcasm shrouded his voice as Rogers swiveled around in the chair to gaze across the bay.

"Well, if you thought we were, you're a dreamer. We're as much prisoners here as they are." Jake's voice carried a weary tone. "Besides, there probably is a prison boss and you can deny it till hell freezes over but I think he's in there right now calling the shots today!"

The warden sighed heavily and lifted the telephone as the noon whistle shrieked. The sun dawdled overhead promising a warm afternoon as the fog drew back a gauzy curtain. Catching Jake on the way from the office, Dan kept in step and said, "Jake, tell me what you know about this man."

Throwing a suspicious look at Dan, Jake said, "Well, you probably know more about this ghost than I do."

"Hey, I've only heard rumors. Is he a convict, guard, visitor?"

"No one knows and all the cons deny it, probably are truthful there because all the inmates don't belong to the elite group, as

I call them. I've seen strange happenings here that can only be explained by the presence of a dictator. He could be a prisoner, guard or someone who visits often like a relative or attorney. I call him Topper because he's above all of us, warden, board and governor. In a strange way, we all answer to him."

As they strolled past the billowing flag slapping the flagpole in a soft breeze, Jake and Dan heard the pleasant clatter of tin plates and the hum of male voices like drones content in their hive.

Dan returned to his office and because he felt a surge of power attributed to the confrontation, decided to handpick his first athlete, Benny, who would be a trainer for future boxers.

A week later, Willie was released from the hospital to resume his spirited ways.

As Dan was walking from his office on this breezy morning, he was deep in thought about the remarks Jake had made after the monthly staff meeting.

"Dan, you don't know how close your tenure was that day in the warden's office."

"Oh, I had an idea."

"Whistler had proposed that the warden terminate you that morning."

"And the warden went for it?"

"Yep. It was the cons, Dan. They made the decision for Rogers."

"You're telling me that I only keep my job at their willy-nilly whim?"

Laughing, Jake looked over in the direction of the cell-blocks, and said, "Something like that. I knew the minute Pigeon showed at the door, you wouldn't be axed."

"Then, there might be a day when they could decide to terminate me?"

"Yep, something like that could happen."

"Jesus! What are you running here?"

" Some people might say it's a prison and we're all prisoners here."

Chapter V

San Francisco
Chinatown 1929

It was early morning with fog hanging low like a gauze curtain obscuring rooftops, as Herbert Angel hurried along the alley. So intent on his mission, he failed to notice the two queue-topped men in silk robes walking nonchalantly toward him until one brushed against him. Startled, he looked into a pair of steely dark eyes as a voice, in perfect English, spoke softly, "Mister Angel, we presume. Would you be kind enough to follow us, sir?"

Angel, whose tongue now stuck to the roof of his mouth in fear, nervously nodded, then turned around and trailed the two men who never glanced back. Watching their queues sway with each step, Angel attempted to recall the reason for the length of their braided hair. Was it a sign of wealth or health? He made a mental note to find out, if he ever lived through this.

The narrow alley, packed with crates and stacked sacks of rice blocked foot passage along the sidewalk to Grant Avenue, forcing them to walk in the middle of the street, dodging vegetable and fish carts pulled by men wearing straw hats and sandals, chanting their wares. As usual, most of the stores in Chinatown had their doors already open despite the early hour and people were hurrying along the sidewalks. In many of the shop windows hung ducks, geese, chickens and rabbits ready to be cooked while in the rear of the shop, their live counterparts were heard squawking and clucking, with annoying swarms of flies flitting everywhere. Over all the foul odors, the sweet, pungent fumes of opium drifted up through the basement stairs. The men now stopped at an apothecary and turned to wait for Angel who was purposely lagging, thinking *it was silly to hurry to his own funeral.*

A bell above the door tinkled when they entered the cramped store. Angel coughed, his lungs threatening to explode from the combination of heat, unwashed bodies and incense mingling with a myriad of strange herbs. The druggist, a short man with a putty face, was intent upon his work, clutching a small bowl and pulverizing pills into a powdery dust covering the counter, never noticed Angel passing by, trailing his two abductors.

Angel knew this shop was particularly popular with the local Chinese due to its unique supply of herbs directly from China. He also knew only too well, the basement opium dens that were still thriving despite the police order to close down. A glass cabinet filled with jars displaying dried sea horses, snakes, crabs, birds and herbs was the druggist's counter. Built into the rear wall were rows and rows of unmarked drawers containing all the mysterious medicines and cures used by the pharmacist. A tiny woman in silk pajamas reaching to her bound feet, was perched high on a stool behind the druggist, warily eyeing all the customers with practiced eye. Angel smiled over at her, knowing that no one would ever be so foolish as to steal from this shop.

The men led Angel toward the rear, sweeping aside rows of elaborately embroidered gowns of silk and satin hanging on racks. For a moment, the men disappeared and Angel looked around admiring the Oriental relics and exquisite art work that rested on delicate teakwood tables or hung on the walls. When the men returned, they motioned Angel to follow them up a steep narrow staircase that creaked loudly, threatening to plunge him into the basement with each hesitant step. Reaching the top landing, Angel saw an open door framing a beautiful Chinese woman in a red satin gown, greeting the men.

They were led into a large airy sunroom in the rear of the flat reeking of incense and smoke, where a rotund man in a satin robe reclined on a large cushion. He was sipping tea and smoking a cigarette held in a long delicately tapered holder while the smoke encircled his head briefly then sifted through the open windows in the rear. Without rising, he greeted Angel, "Ah, Mister Angel, so nice that you found the time in your busy day for a visit."

Angel, clasping his hand, bowed and smiled at the greeting which ignored the fact that he had actually been abducted. "It was you, Mister Chan, who pleased me, sir, by inviting me into your home at a time when you are so busy."

Mister Chan returned the sardonic smile. "Ah, yes. You saw my daughter, Lee, did you?" He was gesturing toward the young woman standing by the door.

"I certainly did, sir. You have much reason to be very proud, with such a beautiful daughter."

The old man smiled, revealing many gold teeth he had acquired while living in Hawaii.

Looking around again, Angel noticed that the young girl had disappeared along with the two goons, which made him more anxious. Feeling sweat accumulate along his forehead but not wishing for the old man to notice, Angel suppressed the urge to reach for a handkerchief.

Nodding happily, the man continued smoking and studying Angel whose tension was mounting. Testing his conscience, Angel could only guess at the one thing he had done that led to this inquisition and he began sweating more. Through the open window, the voices of men hawking delicacies and the aromas that accompanied shark fins, seaweed, bamboo sprouts and aged eggs packed in mud directly from the Chinese mainland, sifted through the morning air making Angel more nauseous.

Finally, Mister Chan rose from his cushion, brushed off his robe and walked over to the door, gesturing to Angel. "Come, we'll go into my office."

In an office packed with relics of every sort along with their stale odors, the man swept papers off the desk and watching as they fluttered to the floor, said in a deliberately low voice, "I am not pleased with you. You have run up such a pile of gambling debts this time. I cannot bail you out."

Despite the calm voice his eyes were blazing as they studied Angel's face, refusing to look away.

"I know," Angel said, feeling weak in the knees and dropping into a wicker chair by the desk. "I tried to stop but it's like that snake over there."

The carved wooden dragon, jeweled eyes gleaming, red tongue flaring, was perched on top of a bookcase. "It's inside my guts! It's eating me alive!"

Chan leaned back in the chair, pushing the loose sleeves of his robe back and studied Angel, saying, "When the dragon enters the body, this is bad." Sighing heavily, he rose and walked to a window, drawing aside the heavy velvet drapes, staring into the street below.

"I can make a certain deal with you that would mark off all your debts."

"I want nothing illegal, Chan." Angel's plea had a hopeful note. "I'll lose my license to practice."

"Or worse, sir, your life. However, this consists of nothing illegal. I'll contact you later, sir."

San Quentin Prison

Dan walked toward death row this morning to visit a condemned man whose execution was pending a call from the governor's office. Angel, hurrying along the sidewalk, joined him, breathless from the fast pace and said, "Hey, Dan, I heard you were promoted, so please accept my heartiest congratulations and condolences!"

"News travels fast around here." Dan said, smiling at his friend's irony.

"Oh, you know the boys. What else is there to talk about?"

"Where are you headed?" Dan asked.

"Aw hell, got to say farewell to one of my losers."

"Getting released?"

"You could say that. He's going to the dance hall in the morning. But what's so damned bad is that his mother wants to attend."

"No."

"That's what the warden said. He refused her request, saying that the publicity is not needed. You can imagine what the press would do with that. Jesus! There's enough trouble here with the murder of Walrus still unsolved, don't you know! The press would hold her hand and yammer about the injustice of it all! Anyway she's having him buried in Boot Hill, if that doesn't make you wonder about her strong maternal instincts!"

"Well, I'll walk with you. That's where I'm going, too."

"Why?"

"Any special needs or last words, I guess."

Dan looked at Angel and then, speaking seriously, said, "I heard that Rogers still thinks hanging's more humane than the proposed gas chamber. Have you heard that?"

"Yeah, I heard that."

"I don't know. Wish we could find a better solution."

"That's it!" Angel exclaimed. "A solution shot into the arm that knocks them into the next world. What about that?"

"That sounds like it is too easy for some of them."

"Well, I don't watch the sideshow anymore. Send one of my flunkies in to hold their hand and curse the state."

By late morning, the fog had snaked across the bay, leaving puffy prints in its wake as the sun poked a hole in the clouds. A pall hung over the prison as usual before an execution and Dan was relieved that it would be the last one of the year. Even though the condemned man was unknown to all of the prisoners and faculty, executions always cast a pall over the entire prison, with an eerie feeling creeping over the walls like moldy vines.

Dan crossed the Porch, entering his office just as the whistle blew announcing the end of the execution and soon prisoners were milling around the yard and working in the gardens. The telephone rang just as he entered the office and Sawbucks yelled, "It's for you, Dan."

"Dan," Jake's voice had an urgent note. "Come over to my office now," and the line went dead.

Jake and Whistler were standing by the windows when Dan entered, greeting him with nods. The atmosphere was strained and before Dan could speak, Whistler exploded, saying, "Where were you anyway?"

"You're speaking of the execution just now? I waited in the cell with the condemned man until the call came in and then went back to my office. Why?"

"The telephone call from the governor came too late, Dan," Jake said. "The con's sentence was commuted to life at the last minute."

With the warden away, the responsibility rested on Whistler's shoulders and as Dan looked at him, he flinched, saying, "What the hell are you looking at? This wasn't my fault! It was the governor's office. The call came too late!"

"Maybe you were in your usual hurry," Jake snapped.

"What the shit does that mean?" Whistler's face was now contorted in anger as he glared at them. "I'm not taking the fall for this, goddammnit! You were there with me this morning! And what about Harry, didn't he rush that rope around the neck before he even looked at the clock? Jeessus! Now that I remember, he skipped over his usual sermon. He must have had a hot date with a plate of roast beef or something!"

"Okay," Jake said. "Let's not get into all that now. First of all, we have to decide what to do."

"Well, the hanging's over and the man's dead." Dan looked at Jake.

"We'll just blame it on the governor's office, that's all." Whistler pursed his lips, eyes narrowing as he considered the situation and said, "Jesus! What will the press do with this!"

"We just tell the truth. It was really no one's fault. We need better communication with the governor's office, that's all."

"Did he have any family other than the mother?" Jake was chewing on a plug of tobacco as he spoke.

"No," Whistler answered. "He's just a street bum in on murder one. He's being buried on Boot Hill."

Walking back to the office Dan glanced toward Boot Hill and reflected on the capriciousness of life, such as a phone call arriving sixty-seconds late.

October arrived without any fanfare except for an unusually large moon that began its pale orbit through the sky, oblivious to earthly events. Icy winds whipped Dan's coat around his legs as he dove into the wind, head tilted. At night, the prison was cloaked in eerie silence with only the moans of the wind mingling with the furtive cries of wandering gulls seeking refuge from the approaching storm.

Cakewalk, the long corridor fronting the execution chamber, was deserted as a lanky guard escorted Dan through the gates toward a building that housed the holding cells for death row inmates prior to their execution. Stepping through the gates into a small vestibule while shaking off the raindrops, he removed coat and cap and handed them to the night guard, "Keyhole" Keats who saluted.

"Howdy, Loot. He's been whining all night, asking for you," he said, nodding toward the cells.

In the half-gloom, staring out of the blackness, the gallows reared stark and somber like a medieval knight in tattered armor crouched low, waiting for the final bugle call. Tonight, Dan shuddered as he passed the room thick with the ambrosia of death corroding the walls and remembered *the damp flesh of her hand in his as she was dying.*

Quickly shaking his head in an effort to douse the memory, Dan walked toward the last cell, saying, "Okay, I'll see what he wants."

"Doc's in there now,"

The sharp-nosed man in a white jacket glanced around in an irritated manner and then plunged a needle into the prisoner's arm.

"Hey!" Willie cried in pain, saying, "Why the hell'd you do that? I gotta talk to the Loot."

"You needed a sedative so you can sleep, Willie." Snapping shut the instrument bag, the doctor nodded coldly in Dan's direction and walked from the cell.

"Is he crazy? Why'd I want to sleep? I'll be sleeping forever in a few hours." Willie was wiping his eyes with a worn shirtsleeve.

Feeling the dampness in the cell penetrate his bones, Dan turned to the guard, saying, "Get some heat in here."

"Why? They're all headed to hell in a few hours anyway. It's a last chance to be cool!"

Seeing Dan's steely eyes, the guard turned and walked out of the cell, saying, "I'll get to it now, sir."

"Loot," Willie, cowering on the cot, sniffed. "I'm glad you came. I need my glasses. Hell, I'm blind without 'em but doc says I don't need to see anymore, anyway."

Dan motioned to the guard standing outside the cell door. "Get his glasses."

"Thanks, Loot. Don't know why they care if I cut my throat now. I'm dying in the morning, anyway. Guess they don't want to clean up the mess," he snickered.

"Okay, Willie, you wanted to see me?"

"Yeah." Willie said, adjusting the round wire-rimmed glasses carefully on his nose, wrapping the shiny tendrils lovingly around protruding ears. "I just wanted you to know I didn't kill ole' Walrus. You've been good to me, Loot. Ever since you kept 'em from flogging me, I been holding a high regard for you, you know."

"You confessed at your trial, Willie. You knew that killing a guard would bring an automatic death penalty."

"Yeah, I know, I know," he said, shaking his head, hands trembling. "But I was picked to get the heat off. Ever since that bull bought the farm, the bulls have been riding us like an entry in a calf roping contest at a rodeo."

"Why were you picked?"

"Aw shit, Loot. I'm so old that I'm already kicking dirt in my grave. What have I got to lose? A few more years here so I'm just switching one hell for another, right?"

"You volunteered?"

"Can I have a cigarette?"

Dan reached into a pocket, drew out a package of Lucky Strikes and lit two, handing one to Willie.

"Was this an order from Topper?"

"I never heard of him." Willie blew smoke through his nostrils, looking across at the guard standing at the door.

"Willie, they can't get to you now."

"Who are they?"

"Okay, let's not play games. I'm thinking there's a prison boss somewhere in or outside these walls, Willie. And if he ordered you to stand trial for his crime of murder then I want him punished. Was he the man who knifed Walrus? Or was he the man ordering it?"

Willie shook his head, casually blowing smoke rings.

"No one can get you here, Willie."

"You kidding? They got the dumb Walrus, didn't they? Right in front of all you screws, too! Yeah, they could get me tonight in this cell. I'd rather die in the gallows than at their hands."

As the sedative took effect, Willie's voice grew weaker, almost inaudible. "Why I wanted to see you Loot, please don't let Croaker do autopsy...." His head began drooping as he struggled for consciousness.

Seeing that Willie was no longer responsive, Dan took the cigarette from limp fingers and, squashing it under his shoe, puzzled over the strange request.

"Get his glasses." Dan said as he walked from the cell, shivering when he stepped out into the wild night while relishing the salty taste of the storm.

The day dawned watery-eyed and soggy after a battering night as the sun weakly peered through a blanket of clouds then abruptly disappeared. The morning still held rumbling thunder and spit long strings of lightning. Pellets of icy rain stung the backs of the four uniformed men, official witnesses, walking toward the building.

"Strange how it always seems to rain on execution day."

"Maybe it's that most executions seem to be scheduled in the winter."

"Yeah."

"I heard it's because the crucifixion of that fella, Jesus, was on a Friday."

"It's supposed to give them hope?"

"Yeah, hoping that the rope will swing 'em far out over the wall!"

53

The men continued with light-hearted banter until they entered the grim building when they quickly sobered in the presence of the death chamber which seemed to reflect the somber appearance of a robed and wigged judge.

Willie was huddled in a corner of the cell, a pile of wrinkled gray laundry. Across from him, a bespectacled man in a dark suit was turning the pages of a book while whispering which resounded in the muted cellblock like a foghorn. Dan stepped into the cramped cell followed by the four witnesses who remained by the door and peered into the dark room.

"Your time is up, Willie," Dan said, thinking, *this never got easier.*

"Loot," Willie pleaded. "Can I wear my glasses in there?"

As the men shuffled their feet, clearing dusty throats, Dan nodded and Keyhole handed over the glasses. At this time, the doctor crept in, followed by the warden and Whistler who lisped, "Why must these dreary occasions be held at the crack of dawn?"

"Good idea," Willie snapped. "Let's do it another time."

"Okay, Willie, let's go." Dan took Willie's arm, guiding him toward the cell door.

"Want a shot, Willie?" Doc was opening his bag.

"See you brought your bag of tricks." Willie said, and, managing a grim smile, "Yeah, a shot of whiskey."

"Don't see why not." Dan looked over at Rogers who nodded approval and the doctor reached into his bag.

Willie gulped the whiskey, then signaling with a wave of his hand, said, "Okay, let's get on with this."

The procession began in the half-light of dawn, rain beating a tattoo on the roof as the men paraded single file led by a chanting chaplain. Dim faces, pale apparitions floating in the air, lined the corridor behind the bars in the cellblock along the route in silent appraisal of the man. However, the sound of a snoring man broke the silence.

In the distance, the haunting notes of a harmonica percolated through the cells, providing a musical score for the whispered intonations of the mumbling minister.

While the prison sat in brooding silence behind a curtain of rain, a hearse, crouched somberly by the iron gates, a black-hooded vulture with folded wings, waited patiently to begin the flight with its prey to a nest high on Boot Hill. A bell tolling in the distance signaled the end of the execution and the arrival of a wooden kimono en route to its earthly bath.

The sky, crayoned with pastel rainbows stretching across the bay, brought a close to Willie's life. Dan remained in his office well into the evening while memories paraded in full dress before his eyes, memories of friends who had died on battlefields for a noble cause and others who died merely to escape life.

Above all, he wondered about the men who court death as fervently and passionately as others court life.

Chapter VI

After arriving at the office on the following morning, Dan was quickly scanning the mail hoping there would be a letter from a club in San Francisco responding to his request for more used athletic equipment when he was greeted by a nervous prisoner who had been waiting for him. An abundant set of protruding teeth stepped across his skinny face as Canary stood by Dan's desk, nervously twisting his cap and shifting from left foot to right.

"Loot, I need to be moved out of the cellblock 'cause Willie's friends are after me."

Dan looked at the prisoner whose reputation for squealing was a festering sore in the cellblocks.

"I'm not surprised. What do you want me to do?"

"Uh, uh, don't know." Canary said, stuttering as his eyes flicked around the busy office.

"Well, I can't move you without proof that you're in danger, Canary." Dan returned to studying the book. Canary stubbornly remained by the desk staring at him until Dan, sighing heavily, set the book down and looked up, asking, "Where are you working these days?"

"The hospital ward, sir."

"Were you there when they brought in Willie's body?"

Canary nodded.

"Was an autopsy performed?"

As his eyes danced around the room, Canary stammered, "I don't know. Maybe, maybe not. I, I, can't remember."

"You can't remember an autopsy being performed?"

"No sir."

"Then, what if I say you're a liar, Canary?"

Shrugging, he said, "Maybe I am, maybe I'm not."

A telephone was ringing across the office and as Dan turned to see if anyone was answering it, he noticed that all the clerks were watching Canary. Later, in relating the incident to his friend, Paddy, Dan noted that "it was a goddamned hostile atmosphere and I should have known not to send Canary back to the cellblocks. Thought that with a little patience, he'd eventually spill what he knew about the doctor."

For long moments the men stared at one another until Canary's eyes shifted and he looked down at his feet. "Ah, Loot, I ain't no squealer."

Dan laughed, saying, "Well, I disagree with you Canary. You've been singing since you arrived here five years ago and you're not about to stop now unless you lose you vocal chords."

Canary shivered, saying, "Yeah, that's it, Loot. I'm in real danger of that."

Dan was serious and asked, "So, if I move you out of the cellblock, you won't have your throat cut. Is that what you're saying?"

"Yeah, I guess."

"Why don't you tell me why Willie's friends want to get you? Is it because you witnessed an illegal autopsy by the doctor? Did he remove anything from Willie's body?"

"Ah, no sir, I seen nothing," Canary said, now becoming agitated as he spoke and nodding his head vigorously.

"If you tell me, I'll protect you."

"Yeah, like you protected Willie."

"He never asked for protection, Canary. If he had informed me about Topper, he'd be alive and Topper would be swinging from that rope and sliced-up by the doc, right?"

Canary turned away from Dan, shaking and trying to focus on the windows, mumbling, "I still say I can't remember."

"Okay." Turning to Sawbucks, Dan signaled with a wave, and said, "Get him a cell in Millionaires Row."

Canary sniveled, saying, "Not there, Loot. They'll know I squealed."

"They think so anyway, Canary. They saw you come in."

Canary stumbled back over the threshold, passing the men without a glance.

Arriving at his office on Monday morning, Dan discovered a shoebox containing a dead canary on his desk.

"Jesus Christ!" Dan slumped into his chair as Sawbucks rushed over. "What the hell's this? Aw hell, Loot, this is some kind of joke. I just saw Canary yesterday heading toward the hospital. He's okay."

"If he's not okay, this is the result of a stupid move on my part," Dan lamented as he took the box and started out the door. "And I hope you're right about Canary."

Doctor Samuel Crockett, prison physician and occasional veterinarian, also referred to as *Croaker* (a name the inmates gave every doctor at the prison since its inception) had been employed at the prison for many years. A tall, wraith-like man whose hawkish nose quivered with each spoken nasal word, Croaker always walked with a deliberate step on rubber-soled shoes as if each movement were painful. The hospital wing was his domain and anyone who entered was considered an intruder and therefore treated like a bug specimen under microscopic examination. His proudest achievements hung in glass frames lining the walls like trophies of a big game hunt. Among these were two degrees from the University of Oxford in England where he had studied in 1914 prominently displayed and it was rumored that although the doctor had sympathized with Germany in the big war, this was never proven.

Rumors circulated throughout the prison about his nocturnal experiments on cadavers but so far no proof of any unethical practices had been shown. The hospital building was called the *Butcher Block* by the convicts whose main preoccupation was to avoid, at all costs, a visit there. Once, several years ago, someone had written on the outer wall, "If you enter here, you will emerge a different man." There was much speculation about the author of that graffiti, with some claiming that he now resided in Boot Hill with various other *bug specimens*.

Dan was fuming as he swung through the door, loudly asking, "Where's Canary?"

"Don't you ever knock?"

"I asked you a question. Where's Canary?"

Looking up from his work, Croaker wrinkled his nose, then, reaching over, waved a paper and said, "I was just filling out his death certificate, if you care to see it." Pausing, as he watched Dan and adding, "People die all the time at a young age, if that's what's bothering you."

Snatching the paper, Dan read aloud, "Heart stoppage! That's a crock of shit! I just saw him on Friday and he was fine. Whining, yet healthy. This is impossible! I want to see the body!"

"Sorry, sent to Boot Hill this morning. The sooner, the better, you know with the chance of spreading a disease and all." The doctor was sucking on a pipe now, puffs of smoke billowing out and clouding his face.

Dan threw the paper on the desk and said, "Then, dig it up, goddamn it!" Slamming the door on his way out he heard the crash of falling glass, turned and saw Croaker's frozen face at the open window.

Rogers' eyes widened as Dan entered the thick-carpeted room without knocking. Motioning to Dan, he leaned back in his chair, saying, "To what do I owe this unexpected visit, and I might add, I do have a telephone." His voice held a note of irritation as he bent to light a cigarette, blowing the smoke directly at Dan.

"I think you know, warden." Ignoring the sarcasm, Dan looked without flinching at Rogers. "You must have received a call by now."

"Oh," Rogers said, chuckling, "you mean the doctor. He did say that you were upset over Canary's death, as indeed, we all are." The smile disappeared as he attempted to show some concern for an inmate he was trying desperately to remember. Then, with a frown, he asked "Wasn't he the little squealer?"

It was Dan's turn to smile now as he studied the warden's face remembering how his friend, Angel, had once described the majority of the prison personnel. *"Shit, Dan, they really believe they're doing mankind a service similar to the dog catcher at the pound who thinks the best dog is a dead dog."*

"Canary didn't die of heart failure, sir." Dan chose to ignore the warden's remark. "He was in good health when I saw him the other day. Also, I found this on my desk this morning." He placed the shoebox containing the dead bird, on the desk.

"So?" Rogers stared into the box. "What's this mean?"

"This is a message, sir. A message loud and clear, that Canary was murdered just as he had predicted when I saw him on Friday."

"He predicted that?"

"Said he'd made some people mad and was afraid his throat would be cut."

"Was it?"

"How the hell would I know? Your doctor had him shoved into Boot Hill over the weekend."

The warden was swiveling in the chair studying Dan, then turned away and concentrated on the windows above Dan's head. For several seconds as Dan patiently waited for a sign that Rogers realized this was a deliberate murder--the murder of a young prisoner as well as one predicted by the victim himself. Then, looking back at Dan, he said with a hopeful note, "Well, men die of heart failure at all ages, Dan."

Dan realized that his battle was just beginning with Rogers, Whistler and all their cohorts lined against him at every move not only in this situation but for any hope of achieving a sports program for the men. Rogers was now displaying the same stone-faced attitude toward the inmates that Dan had seen in the eyes of many guards. Suddenly he felt defeated, like a soldier on the field who lays down his weapon and walks away, uncaring if a bullet finds his back.

Rogers stood and walked to the windows, studying the men working in the garden. "Let me tell you something. This doctor is the finest surgeon in the state. Just look at his credentials.

We're lucky to have him and I don't want anyone upsetting my apple cart, including you."

"Haven't you ever wondered why such a brilliant surgeon is working in a prison for peanuts?"

Heaving a sigh, Rogers turned back from the window and frowned, saying, "I've considered that, but many dedicated people work for purely humanitarian reasons. He fought in the Great War over there, you know, and maybe that brought out a lot of feelings that we wouldn't understand."

"Somehow, he doesn't seem to be a compassionate person. But if you feel that way then you won't have any objection to my request for Canary's body to be exhumed and an autopsy be performed."

"What the hell are you looking for? If his throat was cut, it would be evident, wouldn't it and doc didn't mention that in his autopsy, did he?"

"I just want another opinion on the cause of death other than heart stoppage."

"That entails bringing in another doctor, Dan."

"Yes, I know, the county coroner."

"Are there any relatives listed?"

"Guess not or he wouldn't be booted to Boot Hill."

"I don't know, Dan. This will infuriate the doctor. It's like we're questioning his medical opinion."

"You know, there are rumors circulating about other unauthorized autopsies and nefarious doings happening over there at night."

"You listen to rumors from these cons?"

"Well, I believe there was an autopsy done on Willie, and Canary was a witness. And that's why he was killed. Maybe Canary was blackmailing the doc, or something. Who knows?"

"Willie went to the gallows. No need for an autopsy."

"So why did he have a strange request, sir, that he didn't want an autopsy. Anyway, I believe that Canary's dead because he witnessed an unauthorized autopsy. Or maybe because he didn't try to stop the autopsy."

Rogers looked through the wide windows, staring across at the hospital wing, drumming his fingers on the desk.

"Let's see, Willie was cremated, wasn't he?"

"That's my understanding."

"So, no proof of anything illegal there, would show."

"Canary had the proof if he witnessed an illegal act."

"Okay, call the coroner and get a cemetery detail. I hope I don't live to regret this."

"My hope too, sir."

After Dan walked through the door of the administration building carrying the dead canary, he handed the box to a prisoner working in the flower beds, "Bury this."

The prisoner looked surprised as he doffed his cap and took the box, saying, "Yessir, Loot."

As the inmate grabbed a shovel and started digging, the other workers watched from under their caps as the dead bird was placed gently into the soft earth and buried. Later, when a small cross was discovered on the spot marked *Canary,* the warden ordered it removed.

Chapter VII

San Francisco 1930

Herbert Angel sat by a window in his flat on Telegraph Hill, gazing across at Alcatraz, a federal prison often mistaken for San Quentin, the state prison across the bay. Alcatraz was moored in the middle of the bay like a barnacled, moss-covered whale, with its spouts of light shooting-up the sky and washing away the darkness each night while whistle blasts stung the morning air. Like Angel's losers, it was difficult to ignore and, like them, it held him captive, a fascination he could never explain, even to himself. Representing losers brought little or no money and years of frustration. Maybe it was rooted in his background of poverty and the desperate struggle to complete years of schooling under the most adverse conditions that aroused in him sympathy for others who lacked the ability, talent or strength to achieve any success in life. These were the ones his mother always referred to as "the flotsams and jetsams floating in the stream of life." It was many years before Angel realized their names weren't Flo and Jet.

For Angel, the long struggle was rewarded whenever he witnessed an illiterate bum, having been thrown into jail because he was simply that, and who, after being released, realized that someone cared about him. Of course, more times than Angel liked to admit, the bum repaid with a curse, yet down through the years, he still remained the world's number one sob sister.

He often compared this good Samaritan feeling for the indigent to his insatiable appetite for food which also was rooted in those hungry years of youth when there was never enough food on the table to obliterate the rumblings of an empty stomach.

Turning away from the view, he glanced at a letter received in this morning's mail. *Probably one of his losers threatening to sue,* he was thinking while tearing open the envelope. Scanning the page, his eyes narrowed as he flipped over the envelope searching for a return address. No luck, and shit! It was written in Cantonese! Herbert Angel, barrister, was worried. His conscience dictated that this must be a threat and he needed a translator, which posed a problem. What's in the letter and would he want anyone else to read it? It could be very incriminating, costing his job or even worse, especially if it was from Mister Chan, rumored to be the leader of one of the cruelest tongs in Chinatown. Known as the *highbinders,* they actually used hatchets and cleavers when enforcing their own laws within the confines of Chinatown which to Chan was a separate country within the enclave of the city.

Angel was always fond of telling anyone who would listen that his journey on this planet had been spent climbing a series of broken rungs on the ladder of life. So now, he decided, this predicament proved that to be true because he was back in the basement of life again. Leaning back in the chair, he lit another cigar wondering if he should ride over on the ferry to the prison today or send an underling. It promised to be another day spent either in a courtroom defending the indigent or trotting across the bay to one prison or the other, interviewing, consoling and coddling life's losers.

The irony of his job, however, was that he was as big a loser as any of his clients since gambling had sprouted long tentacles that had become embedded in his very soul. Like the alcoholic, Angel tried but couldn't shake his addiction. Betting on the Chinese lotteries had been fascinating in the beginning when he was caught up in the excitement of winning but it could also be deadly if he reneged on a bet. Angel was personally acquainted with the few unlucky souls who failed to ante-up on a bet. They simply disappeared after being seen strolling through the streets of Chinatown in the company of some very fat, silk-robed men with queues down to their asses and short daggers dangling from wide belts.

After that unexpected and scary visit with Chan, Angel had tried to keep his gambling habit under control by limiting visits into Chinatown. As Angel had watched, Chan had marked off those heavy debts he owed in the lottery and with a handshake, promised to get in touch later. Sighing heavily, the perpetual jovial look faded into a scowl as he folded the letter and placed it into the briefcase. He remembered the little Chinese thief in prison who could decipher this letter, if he felt like it. That was the damned problem with those people, independent as hell!

He rose from the chair, shooting another glance through the window at the prison, walked across the room to a hall mirror and placed the bowler on his head, noticing new worry lines creasing his brow. Shrugging into a coat and scarf, he grabbed the heavy briefcase and set out to face the day, hoping he wouldn't meet any fat, silk-robed men with long queues and cleavers along the way.

It had been a quiet weekend at the prison and on this Monday morning while entering the office, Dan was thankful for just that small respite. No escape attempts, no hunger strikes and no murders, so far. He was also aware of the rumors spreading through the walls like the low murmur of a distant surf. These men with their odd senses knew that Dan was agitating for a sports arena inside and, somehow, this information seemed to calm them, temporarily.

"Where the hell's Benny?" Dan was reaching for a coffee cup when he looked around the office.

"Whistler came in on Friday after you left, Dan," Sawbucks said, frowning. "He said that Benny hadn't served his time in the jute mill."

"He's in the jute mill?"

"Guess so."

Slamming the cup on his desk, Dan grabbed his cap and started through the door as the office staff waited in eager anticipation for another encounter with the brass.

Rogers, Whistler and Croaker, labeled *The Magi*, by the inmates, were seated around the desk when Dan entered the warden's office. Rogers, a product of North Dakota, was a former sheriff and dedicated lawman, instilled by ancestors to quietly endure a hard-scrabble life in the ice-encrusted desolate mountains. "However, lady luck, that wonderful commodity which eludes most people, gave me a stamp of approval while panning for silver in Nevada," he delighted in relating to anyone interested.

"After striking a lode, he was appointed sheriff in the Reno area. In those times, high positions in law enforcement were plums to be purchased rather than earned," Jake had informed Dan during one of their early briefings.

"Whistler's an enigma," Jake said, "because no one's sure about his background. Some heard he arrived as a guard years ago and others claim he arrived with another warden and stayed until Rogers appointed him chief flunky."

While Dan surveyed the trio who struck him as a tribunal of negative justice, he recognized the familiar looks of disdain and maybe even a bit of veiled envy on the part of Rogers who had once opined that it's an absolute impossibility to be a friend to a convict.

"It's a sign of weakness and an open invitation to get your throat slit," he often said.

Whistler waved a paper in the air, saying, "We have a letter here from a board member who claims it was sent by you."

"Let me see." Dan walked across to the desk and studied the paper, then nodded, "Yep, looks like my signature. What's the problem?"

Whistler scoffed. "What's the problem? Hear that, warden? This man has no conception of the problems that have arisen since his arrival here."

Dan looked in amazement at the man who made no pretense of his feelings toward Dan, often mimicking the prisoners' reference to him as The Loot.

Rogers was speaking in a calm voice, saying, "This letter, Dan, is a request for a baseball field and boxing ring and was sent to the board without my approval."

"I know. That's what it is, for sure."

"You've gone over our heads!" Whistler exploded.

"No, I wasn't aware of that fact. It was a simple request for an important problem that you've been ignoring all this time and I've taken it up with you many times. If you don't want any more strikes, hunger or otherwise, you have to keep these men occupied while they're in lockups and crowded exercise yards."

Rogers nodded, saying, "You're right, Dan. But a sports program is out of the question. Can't you see what the people of this state would say if they heard these murderers and thieves were enjoying sports like any other honest law-abiding citizen? Jesus! They'd have my goddamned tail, I know that." By now, his red face matched Whistler's as he pounded a fist on the desk. "When they walked through those gates out there, they relinquished all their goddamned civil rights, including playgrounds!"

Dan remained stubbornly by the desk and said, "So what has the board decided?"

"You don't get it, do you? Just don't get it!" Whistler now took a package of cigarettes from his pocket while Rogers was speaking and, fumbling for a match, blew a cloud of smoke over Croaker who fanned it away from his face, throwing an irritated look at Whistler. "The board has decided to suspend you until further notice."

In the silence, Croaker coughed nervously. "I think that's a little too sudden, Whistler, don't you?"

Rogers rose from the chair and ignoring Whistler, looked at Dan as he spoke. "The board has given me the option and I have decided to ignore the infraction this time, Dan. But in the future, any requests for a program of any kind for the men or a request for any equipment must be channeled through my office."

Turning toward the door, Dan spoke firmly, glaring at Whistler, saying, "Oh, by the way, I want Benny returned to my office this afternoon," and strode through the door while the men looked on in amazement.

"What nerve!" Whistler crushed the cigarette in an ash tray, saying, "That will happen over my dead body!"

Croaker looking keenly at him, said, "Where do you want to be buried, in Boot Hill or in town?"

"What the hell does that mean?"

"It means," Croaker sighed, "that if Benny's not returned, we face another week of strikes, believe me."

Rogers picked up the telephone, and ordered Benny's transfer from the mill back to Dan's office.

While studying the rap sheet at Benny's booking, Dan learned that Benny had been an abandoned baby found on the steps of a church and raised in an orphanage until his career began as a Golden Glover, gaining fame while barely out of childhood. The boxing ring became his home, the leather gloves his family, and the peal of a bell answered quicker than his peers answered school bells. Despite a short stature, his physique was more worthy of a lumberjack than a snappish kid, cultivated and harrowed in city beds of concrete. An officer, placing handcuffs on the bloody fists, had written in his report, "The fighter had beaten his wife to death in a scene so indescribable that an autopsy had to be performed to determine the age and sex of the corpse. When we arrived, Benny was standing over a mound of flesh in the blood-spattered room, kicking the corpse and punching air, sweat drenching his face, saying, "Hey, the bell ain't wrung yet, ref!"

"The jury should have found the poor slob insane," Sheriff Bob Riley said, as Dan joined him for coffee in the officer's mess after the booking. "Instead they gave him life without parole. It beats me!"

Dan looked at the sheriff and said, "Well, maybe it's a break for me."

"For you? Why?"

"You'll see."

The sheriff looked puzzled. "I hope you're not still agitating for the sport of boxing in here, Dan."

"Good idea!"

"Shit! He's liable to kill the first guy you put in the ring with him."

"Benny? No, he won't."

"Why are you so confident?"

"Because if Benny ever kills again, it will be his wife."

"You mean the dead one?"

"That's right." Dan looked thoughtful as he lifted the cup of coffee. "He's filled with remorse over it."

"Sorry he killed her?"

"Yeah, wants to apologize. Says he should have finished her off quickly, not let her suffer like that."

"So, you're saying he wants to do it over but quicker."

"Yep."

"Then the guy's nuts, like I said!"

"Or else, he's compassionate."

The sheriff snorted, saying, "You gotta be nuts to work here."

Dan laughed, saying, "And your line of work is better?"

"Yes, in the way that I'm not locked inside a walled fortress with a few thousand crazies."

As they shook hands in parting, Sheriff Riley said, "I have to hand it to you, Dan. Your perseverance for sports in here will pay off someday, I predict."

"Thanks for your vote of confidence."

When Benny arrived at the office on the following morning, Sawbucks was as surprised as the office staff who looked to see what the Loot's reaction would be. Dan continued reading the prison paper, not looking up as Benny brought his morning coffee and returned to the file cabinets in the next room.

The only disturbance in the prison that morning was the discovery of a dead frog flattened on the doctor's chair in the hospital wing.

"What the shit is this?" Croaker yelled the minute he sat, jumping back and waving his arms. "Somebody get this thing out of here!"

An orderly rushed over and, placing the frog in a paper bag, walked through the hospital toward the bay where he tossed it over the stone wall. A flock of gulls swept out of the fog and trumpeting their arrival with loud squawking and flapping wings surrounded the prisoner in a vain attempt to snatch the tasty morsel out of his hand. In the hospital ward, a sound of croaking rose from the beds where several hundred men were being treated for dysentery, pneumonia and various diseases.

At the staff meeting later that afternoon with Whistler, Jake and Dan, Croaker complained of the incident. "What the hell does that damned message mean?"

Whistler darted a look through the window at a group of inmates gathered on the lawn. "Have no idea. The last time something like this happened, Canary died."

"I had nothing to do with his death, Whistler, and you know it!" Croaker said, shaking with anger.

Jake, looking over at Dan as he spoke, raised his eyebrows and said, "We haven't decided yet how Canary died, right Dan?"

Croaker looked surprised and said, "He died from a bad heart."

"Well, the body's with the coroner in town."

"Who ordered that?" Croaker angrily asked.

"Rogers." Dan spoke quickly, "We all believed that his death was very strange, that's all."

"Well, no one told me." Croaker sounded both angry and hurt. "He's questioning my abilities as a doctor?"

The air in the room was crackling until Whistler said, "Well, I'll look into this dead frog thing, anyway. With Rogers away, I'm the acting warden, you know."

"How long's Rogers going to be away?" Croaker's hands were shaking.

Whistler shrugged, saying, "Just two days," and tossing a glance across at Dan and Jake, added,. "I guess that's all for today. See you next week."

As the men were leaving the room, Whistler summoned his clerk, saying, "Find out what the hell's going on out there on the lawn and get their numbers!"

The prisoner glanced through the window then hurried from the room as Whistler watched the group disappear quickly when they spied the young convict, knowing that an order from Whistler usually brought solitary confinement.

Smiling now, Whistler turned back to the desk and began writing out fresh orders.

"I see no difference in the intellect among those who come willingly to walk the walls here and those who come reluctantly to vegetate in the cells," Whistler commented in an interview on a San Francisco radio station later in the week. This remark did not go unnoticed by both guards and prisoners, especially Informer, the newspaper editor, who wrote, "We, who vegetate in cells here, however reluctantly, can only sympathize with the brass who must endure the presence of ignorant guards on a daily basis in order to keep all of the vegetables in line."

In the years since Dan's arrival, the prison population had grown steadily, credited by many to the country's economic conditions which had gradually worsened, causing many otherwise honest men to resort to drastic measures in order to feed their families. With the state providing financial assistance for families of the incarcerated, word quickly spread and many who never would consider committing a criminal act, were shackled and led through the iron gates.

"It's a rat cage in here!" Roller Skates complained one day while on guard duty in the officers' mess. "They're standing on shoulders in the yard and pissing on feet. I sure ain't going into that yard out there without a weapon! So I got assigned here for all my bitching!"

"You have a weapon," Dan said, looking irritated, "your feet!"

"Not funny." Roller Skates lit a cigarette while leaning against a wall by the door, watching servers. "So, I hear the hen house will be closing down soon."

"That's the rumor. Heard any more?"

Shrugging, he said, "No, not any more than that surprise letter from the board last summer asking us for suggestions for its use."

"It'll be a helluva relief to get rid of those women." Dan said, finishing his lunch of steak and fries as he looked through the window toward the Hen House.

"Yeah," Skates said laughing, "Remember the time that crazy Joe Kidd hid out in their laundry room?"

"He sure as hell wasn't thinking when he dropped into that cage of angry women!"

"Yeah, thought he'd get something for nothing."

The incident had occurred about two years before and was bandied around the prison for months, each time becoming more embellished until it had assumed ridiculous proportions. The women supposedly had ripped-off his pants and repeatedly raped him was the popular belief, which Joe happily encouraged. In actuality, after crawling through the vent in the ceiling and dropping into the steaming room where several women were at work doing the laundry, he was surprised to discover the women prisoners were indistinguishable in appearance from their matrons, with no craving desire to see why he was there.

By the time he was mercifully rescued by some matrons who had rushed into the laundry at the sound of his howling, Joe wasn't able to explain his presence. Later, when the women's version of his trapeze act was related, the humiliation of their rejection was almost as painful as the physical assault. One woman had poured hot water over his head while two others held him down, stripped off his pants and struck him on each bare cheek with a hot iron.

"Yeah. The poor guy did a long stretch in the hospital and had trouble walking for a long time!"

"A good specimen for the Croaker, don't you think?"

Skates joined in the boisterous laughter as other guards looked over curiously.

"They were a good riddance!"

The women's prison had occupied an old building by the seawall almost since the beginning days of the prison. Roosting by the bay in silent dignity and only an arm's reach from the beehive cluster of drones, the Hen House remained aloof and alone. Taken out for exercise when the men were locked into their cells at night, the women wearily trudged along the board sidewalk through the small village and back to their cells, so quietly that the only sound the villagers ever heard was an occasional cough or giggle.

Called into the Hen House once, Dan later reflected at a staff meeting, saying, "It was like walking into a rabbit warren; women wandering through the halls, listless and bored with no regimen for them to follow."

Rogers nodded, adding, "You know, most women prisoners are not hardened criminals, just sort of sad creatures. Their crimes are mostly of a personal nature, like the murder of a relative or lover. After they serve their term, they're usually never seen again."

Jake agreed. "Sure as hell isn't what we face, with these damned mean repeaters. Don't have to be in law enforcement to know they're impossible to control."

"Too bad they couldn't have an exercise program." Dan looked around the long table as the other members who pretended not to hear, glanced away.

"Hey, Dan, don't you ever give up?"

"Not as long as I'm alive, Jake." Dan cast a side glance across the table at Whistler who had buried himself in a raft of papers, ignoring the remarks.

After the announcement of the impending closure of the Hen House, a surprised Informer wrote poignantly,

"The Hen House will soon be barren but we, the male occupants of this lost expanse of desert, would lay our heads once more upon a warm bosom; would suckle the milk of a woman's love and knead her sweet flesh. Alas, to the world they are women scorned but to us, they are maidens of hope in an impoverished land of despair. For even a brief glimpse in passing of a woman's soft face has bridged the endless days and alienated nights. Farewell, sweet princesses, sweet dreams! We are now truly without gingham or guns!"

Early one morning, as the women marched in a single line through the black iron gates, spilling into large yellow buses like schoolgirls going to a prom, guards cheered and inmates jeered. Cloudy billows of dust rose, hovering over the yard where the women had been assembled, obscuring the sunlight as the chattering women waved a farewell, some holding their noses, others using obscene gestures toward the guards while blowing kisses to the viewing prisoners.

"The hell hags have left the brooder and the barnyard now can rest in peace." Sawbucks said, watching the last vehicle disappear into the landscape and taking a deep breath he turned back to his job inside the walls.

Dan watched from the front office as the yellow buses pulled away, spewing fumes, driving toward their final destination on a sand-crusted desert far away.

Rogers who joined Dan at the windows, fumed. "They never belonged in such close proximity to men whose libidos are also caged, for God's sake! A boy locked inside a candy store can at least break the glass-covered trays."

"Yeah," Dan said, laughing, "Ask poor old Joe about breaking and entering!"

Rogers joined in the laughter, "Forgot about that!"

The dust hadn't settled from the evacuation of the women before others were coveting the empty Hen House. Almost immediately, Dan accosted Rogers in the corridor one morning as Rogers was rushing to a meeting with the board.

"I know, Dan. I know why you stopped me but I have already reserved that space for Croaker's hospital."

"That's fine but there's enough room for a gymnasium also, don't you think?"

"You're trying to turn this place into a country club Dan, and I don't like it. Anyway, a better hospital is more important right now."

"Okay, I have an idea. Why don't we ask the men?"

Whistler approached as they were talking and said, "What's he asking for now, Rogers, a new golf range?"

"No. I just wanted one golf ball and a tee!"

Rogers laughed and said, "Even that's asking too much these days, Dan."

When he learned of the stalemate, Informer posed the question of gymnasium or hospital extension in his next edition. Ignoring the officials, the prisoners took their own vote and the gymnasium won. A livid Croaker promised to take this matter to the state legislature. "The men only want a place to play. What happens when they become very seriously ill? Where will they go?"

Informer printed his letter in the following edition and the prisoners were overwhelming in their response: "Where we usually go, Croaker, to Boot Hill!"

The final editorial on the subject was written by an irate Informer: "We, the populace of this great institution which is, by the way, still self-supporting, wish to inform the state and all its personnel far and wide that if it weren't for us, you would be jobless, standing in one of those long unemployment lines on some deserted street corner, selling apples. So, let us have our gymnasium!"

"Are they threatening us?" Sawbucks threw down the paper as he looked across the room at the busy men who never managed to look him in the eye, and shivered.

Dan laughed and said, "Well, telling us that we'll be out of work if they decide to go straight, is a novel idea, don't you think? Anyway, Informer hit a sore spot when he wrote of those long unemployment lines."

The board had the final word. Croaker's hospital was to be enlarged to contain a better equipped operating room and Dan received the vague promise of a meeting at some future date. At the next staff meeting, Whistler, joining the others at the table, looked across at Rogers and said, "Well, warden, I think we should prepare for another hunger strike. Thanks to the Loot, the men are restless!"

"I see no sign of restlessness in the men. Informer was only expressing an opinion, not calling for a strike." Rogers glared back at Whistler and said, "So, let's get on with the business of running this booby hatch."

Chapter VIII

Despite the setback, through the following months, Dan pursued his goal for a sports program to be introduced into the prison. He sent letters to the legislature and spent weekends in San Francisco, visiting local ball clubs while enlisting aid from their coaches and sponsors.

At the local gyms, he contacted boxing managers and began collecting uniforms, gloves and shoes, while receiving promises of exhibition games at the prison in the future. On Friday nights, Dan could be found in the audience, enjoying the boxing matches, especially the Golden Gloves, and obtaining invaluable assistance in the training of boxers and wrestlers. On a few of these occasions, Angel joined him at the arena and then a quick stop at Paddy's home for a shot of his imported whiskey before the trip back to the prison.

Dan had hoped the two men would become friends but somehow, they kept their distance, sharing only an occasional visit when Dan insisted.

"What's with this?" Dan had once asked Paddy. "You and Angel don't seem to be very friendly, and that's bothered me."

"Well, Danny," Paddy got that faraway look in his eye again, saying, "We're on opposite sides of the tracks remember?"

"Sure, so am I."

"He's not really admired in the legal circles here in the city. There have been rumors of his connection with the Chinese tongs, for one thing."

"Oh, shit! He's talked a little about his gambling but that's all it amounted to. It's no more a problem than a man's drinking, is it?"

"That's not what I hear, Danny."

Dan decided that if he wanted to visit with his friends occasionally, it would have to be at separate times. Then one day, Paddy inquired, "How's your friend, the con's advocate, doing these days?"

Noticing the unusually concerned tone in his voice, Dan looked at Paddy, asking, "Why? Heard something?"

Paddy shrugged and said, "No. Just didn't want you to think I would be so bold as to disapprove of your friends."

Dan laughed, saying, "Never crossed my mind, Paddy."

With that unspoken apology, Angel once again became a guest at Paddy's home for a shot of whiskey after the boxing matches.

"Sure glad I don't have to catch the ferry back to that dungeon tonight." Angel was watching the ferry slip into its berth as the three men stood on the wharf one autumn evening. "But you know, somehow I have a feeling you don't agree."

Dan shook his head. "You'd never understand my reasons for being there so I won't waste my breath explaining."

During the ferry ride, Dan wondered about Angel who was so preoccupied these days that his cheerful disposition seemed to have evaporated.

The rising sun silhouetted the horizon while leaves skipped along the sidewalk, chattering underfoot. Standing on the porch, Dan watched the prisoner shuffling along the walk in a strange gait like a puppet whose twisted strings were being tugged in every direction, stopping occasionally to wipe his nose on a shirt sleeve and mumbling, "Damned if I don't, dead if I do."

"Damned if you don't what?" Dan's voice startled the prisoner who drew back, saying, "Oh."

Then Bags stopped and saluted, "Hi, Loot, ah, nothing, sir."

"Coming to see me?" Dan asked.

Bags hesitated as he noticed the men pruning bushes were staring at him.

"No sir," he shouted and hurried down the path.

Puzzled over the inmate's odd behavior, Dan remembered when Bags had been booked a few years ago. Sheriff Riley had removed the cuffs from the youth while handing the papers to Dan. "Kid's a goddamned mess, right, Bags?"

For a moment, Dan recognized the familiar flash of fear pass through the youth's eyes, then the hardness returned as he spit at Riley who immediately cuffed him across the mouth, yelling, "Rotten mangy cur!"

After the sheriff had departed, Dan scanned the rap sheet while Sawbucks was assigning his cell and jute mill hours.

Emerging from a rebellious youth spent on city streets dodging bullets and brass buttons, Bags eventually entered prison at the age of eighteen on the arm of his father who was given a death sentence for the murder of a policeman in the course of a robbery. A life sentence for aiding and abetting in the robbery by driving the getaway car had, in time, sobered Bags.

"Hey, Loot, I ain't gonna be no trouble maker here. If I do good time in the mill, can I get a break some day?"

Dan kept an eye on Bags, sensing under the brazen veneer a frightened young man who, as a runaway from an orphanage at the age of ten, was raised on the city's hardpan streets and empty lots by a menagerie of petty criminals and stray cats.

Trusting in his judgment of men, Dan eventually assigned Bags to the farm where the benefits were less fencing and more freedom, bunk beds in a barn in lieu of iron beds in a cell, a cowboy on a ranch instead of a criminal in a cell, and the smell of horseflesh over the odors of male sweat.

The horseflesh on the farm consisted of a lone, bandy-legged nag of questionable vintage used for plowing the many vegetable gardens. The bond between man and beast was the shared life sentence imposed upon both. Each morning as Bags washed and brushed the old horse in preparation for the day's work, he could be heard whispering promises of a better life while the old nag chewed on the sugar lumps. When suffering a ribbing by other inmates, Bags merely grinned and said, "You guys don't know what it's like having a dumb animal for a friend."

"Yeah, Bags, we do. Ain't you our friend?"

The thought of losing this one bright spot in his miserable life terrified Bags who said, "Goddamned, if I ever lose this job, I'll just die."

By late afternoon, the trees were cowering in the autumn heat with an occasional breeze fanning the prison. Dan, still puzzling over Bags and his strange behavior that morning had an eerie premonition that something wasn't right and decided to send a messenger out to the farm.

"Tell Bags I want him in my office by four," Dan said as an anxious Pigeon eagerly responded, stuttering, "Yessir."

Walking through the stalls in the barn and hearing muffled sounds coming from the last stall, Pigeon was greeted by a sight that he later said, "Thought Bags was playing a joke on me the way he was hanging there, kind of upside down over that ole' nag!" Bags was hanging from a beam, body bouncing against a post and still twisting in the air over the form of a dying horse sprawled in the sawdust, thrashing and snorting.

When Dan arrived, he found Croaker bending over the inert body listening for a heartbeat.

"Looks like Bags rode the old pinto into the sunset," he joked, rising to his feet and stuffing the stethoscope into his black bag.

Bags' room in the barn had already been searched and Dan glanced around expecting a suicide note or some explanation for the cruel death of the convict's beloved animal.

"Are you saying suicide?"

"Hell, yes. Self-evident! He placed the rope around his neck, positioned the horse, climbed on the old nag's back after giving the horse some poisoned sugar cubes and waited for the horse to collapse, then bingo!"

"You have this neatly figured out, don't you? Somebody else could have done this, you know." Dan was feeling angry and frustrated.

79

"True. But why? Was this little creep that important to someone?"

"Well, that's for us to find out, don't you think?" As he turned to leave, Dan frowned, saying, "How do you know the horse was poisoned? He could have died of old age considering that he's been here for years."

"I'm just guessing but I've also been a student of animal husbandry."

"Why doesn't that surprise me? By the way, I want Bags taken to the coroner in town."

"What?" Croaker yelled. "Who the hell are you to decide that? I have to do an autopsy."

"An autopsy will be done, but not by you, if I have any say about it." Dan strode from the barn with Croaker trailing, hollering, "You goddamned don't have any say in this. I'll have the last say!"

Prisoners arriving to put the body on a stretcher were openly gawking as the two men walked through the barn with Croaker ranting and trailing Dan who calmly climbed into a waiting car with Sawbucks at the wheel, asking, "What the hell's he yelling about?"

"Seems to think he has a right to do an autopsy and I disagree."

"Bags is dead?" Sawbucks turned incredulous eyes on Dan who simply nodded, saying. "Yep. He was found hanging, actually dangling over the old horse. Another strange death, if you ask me."

Along the southern edge of the farm, a shoulder blade of the prison jutted over the edge of the bay, shrugging long shadows across the water with no trespassing signs dotting the landscape. An armed guard's tower, a crusty scab on the stone walls, warned any approaching pleasure craft to stay away.

Near fading hills peppered with dandelion and creeping poison ivy, a line of small colorful cottages like late blooming flowers, hemmed the western edge of the fortress, spilling over into a small valley. These were the manicured homes of the employees' families whose gardens were carefully nurtured by prisoners who took immense pride in their work. One year this was mentioned in the city newspaper as an example of landscape painting at its best. Informer filled a page with this in his weekly editorial, comparing the prison grounds to a trip through Monet land. All that's missing is the river that borders the gardens, flowing gently into the bay.

Adjacent to the homes and seemingly incongruous in this grim setting, a small red-roofed, twin-gabled school house, appearing to be torn from a fable's page, stretched its arms to embrace a large tree-shrouded playground sloping to well-worn tennis courts.

As the entourage carrying the body wound through the pastoral scene, passing by the schoolyard, small children gathered along the fence to watch.

Later that day while foghorns on the bay still belched warnings, Dan watched a jittery Jiggs limping awkwardly toward his office, pausing briefly to remove a cigarette balanced precariously on the tip of one ear. As he lit it, he glanced back in that familiar gesture of a prisoner's abiding fear of a knife in the back, literally.

Time had etched patterns across his leathered face, each line crisscrossing the easel as if engraved by a finely-honed chisel. Deep crevasses were hollowed along the cheeks and when he smiled, a host of rivulets spilled from the edges of his jaw, emptying into the cheeks.

"Loot," Twisting a worn gray cap in both hands, Jiggs stood by Dan's desk, hopping from one foot to the other as he spoke in a pleading tone, "I been in here almost twenty years now and ain't been no stoolie. I did my time in the Hole, too!" The latter was pronounced with a note of pride.

Dan nodded, leaning back in the chair and waited for the nervous prisoner to continue.

Jiggs hesitated, looking over at Sawbucks, who, sensing the situation, offered, "I'm going for coffee, Dan. Want some?"

Dan shook his head and continued studying the inmate as he said, "Well, he's gone, now what?"

"Gonna be a big break, Loot and you're a target," pausing to catch his breath, "along with me." Jiggs continued shifting his weight from one leg to the other as he took another deep breath.

While absorbing the prisoner's words, Dan was conscious of the whirring ceiling fan squeaking in the quiet office.

"Loot," he said, face twitching. "I'm scared."

"Of what?"

"They're gonna grab a con and a bull, er sorry, I mean you, sir, so it'll confuse the bulls."

"Why are they after you?" Dan became interested at this point, thinking that it's true as Jake once said, working here makes a person suspicious of any action or reaction by a convict.

"Don't know. Guess 'cause I'm on the back gate, sir."

"Okay, when's this coming-out party going to take place?"

"Don't know, Loot."

"You're on the back gate?"

"Yeah."

"What hours?"

"Early morning shift."

"Okay," Dan rose, gathering up some papers on the desk and gesturing to the inmate, still frozen to the spot and said, "That's all."

"That's all, Loot? Ain't you gonna phone or something?"

"What do you think I should do?"

"Maybe take a vacation?"

"And take you with me?"

"Good idea, sir."

For several minutes they studied one another, the inmate with a long record and the cagey officer who had weathered many fabricated stories, now feeling slightly dubious about this one.

When Sawbucks returned, carrying a thermos of coffee and almost colliding with Jiggs in the doorway, he looked over at Dan, who asked, "Why would an inmate risk certain death to warn me of an impending escape attempt?"

"He did that?"

Dan related the conversation as they shared coffee and ideas. "Doesn't make sense, maybe it's a trap," Sawbucks sipped hot coffee with a worried look. "Something else might be in the works."

"That occurred to me. But what if Jiggs is telling the truth and is scared for himself knowing that once outside the walls, he'll be killed? He's also aware of Bags' fate and probably knows more about that than he'll ever tell."

"You don't believe Bags killed himself, do you?"

"No. Bags had some information, dangerous information and that's why he died. Just wish I knew what it was."

Staring at the wall while lost in thought, Dan wrinkled his forehead. "You know, somehow I see the fine hand of that ghost, Topper, or someone like him in this."

"It's a puzzle, all right, but I don't think Topper gets involved in escape plans, if there is such a guy. You know, once I found some old sketches of the original prison layout and believe it or not, there's lots of holes and crannies down in that area where the dungeon is, that haven't been explored. That place could be a great place for a ghost to hide!"

Dan, glancing over to see if Sawbucks was joking but his face was a map of thoughtfulness, said, "Hey, if you're a ghost, you don't need to hide!"

Sawbucks laughed. "Good thought there, Dan. But, you know, it could be a good place for a con to hide out."

As they continued sipping coffee and smoking, a radio in the office began a medley of Christmas music, saluting the season which was still a few months away.

Suddenly, Dan rose from the chair, grabbed his cap and shouted, "I'll be back in about an hour."

"Where are you going?"

"I'm going to see a man about a horse!"

Dan stood in the warden's office, holding a large book, waiting for Rogers, as Jake and Whistler entered the room.

"Saturday afternoon," Whistler steamed. "This had better be important. I had to cancel a golf game with the warden."

Jake exchanged glances with Dan, curiosity edging his voice, "Problems in the cell blocks, Dan?"

"No," Dan said, watching as Rogers strode through the door, "I'm sorry about the cold room but the repairman for the furnace is ill. Maybe we can find another."

"Find another repairman? Or find another room?" Rogers sounded peeved.

"Repairman, sir," Dan smiled.

"Well, it's freezing in here! Whistler, find someone now!"

"I'll call, sir."

"The hell you will! You find someone now!"

"But don't you want me here for the meeting?"

"Oh, for Chrissakes, go!"

As Whistler hurried from the office, Rogers turned to Dan. "What the hell is going on? This is Saturday afternoon and my golf game had to be cancelled."

"This won't take long, sir." Dan motioned them to a chair as he held up a book.

"What the hell! Greek mythology?" Jake sounded leery.

"That's right," Dan turned to an underlined page. "It's the tale of a Trojan Horse. So, with the holidays coming, I have a Christmas story that you'll enjoy. While I was away, Bags stopped by my office on the day of his death and dropped-off this book from the library. Until today, I had no idea what it meant but now it's clear to me."

Watching Jake and Rogers, Dan saw their curiosity was aroused as they listened.

"I know that Bags loved the mythologies, even called the old nag on the farm Aristotle. Well, what happened in that story? An army hidden within a wooden horse drew up to the gates of a walled city and the curious citizens opened the gates, falling into the hands of their enemy."

"Yes, yes, what has this to do with us?" Rogers seemed more impatient than puzzled.

"On Christmas morning for the past few years, the inmates have staged a sleigh ride through the grounds to the back gates distributing candy and fruit to the children here. And," Dan said, looking over at Rogers, "you approved the use of the old horse on the farm with Bags disguised as Santa Claus."

"Yes. We decided it would establish better relations between the guards and prisoners."

Dan nodded, saying, "And so far, it has."

Rogers beamed as he reached for a cigarette, leaning back in the chair. "And the sleigh ride is scheduled again for this year."

In the quiet room, Dan watched their faces, wondering if they were getting his point. "Bags was trying to warn me without being a stoolie, I believe. Maybe he was being watched, I don't know. When he returned to the barn after leaving my office, he either committed suicide, taking his friend with him, as Doc claimed. Or, he was murdered by someone who suspected that he was about to squeal, which is my theory. But it will be hard to prove and maybe we'll never know."

"Bags and the horse are dead," Rogers stated flatly.

"I know, but when Jiggs, who's a trustee on the back gate, came to me with the news of an escape plan, I remembered Bags also had once been a cellmate of Jiggs. Haven't you replaced the horse on the farm and won't the ride be scheduled again this year?"

"Goddammn!" Rogers collapsed in the chair as Jake let out a low whistle.

"Now you see. I had the furnace sabotaged because for some strange reason, I didn't want Whistler to hear about this and don't ask me why. Maybe it's because he always seems to talk too much. Don't know how but the inmates seem to know his every move. Anyway, this plan of theirs, ingenious as it is, can be used to our advantage. Allow them to go on with their plan or otherwise we'll never know who's involved."

"Good idea." Jake smiled.

"What about weapons?" Rogers raised his eyebrows. "Do you think they might have weapons?"

"I thought of that. If they do, we can overcome them before they reach the back gates. Probably grab them when they first begin loading the men into the sleigh."

"Yeah, and that'll be at the commissary getting the supplies." Jake seemed pleased with this thought.

"Right on," Rogers agreed. "So I won't say a word to Whistler?"

"I wouldn't, sir."

Dan was returning to his office just as a prisoner rushed by with a tool box, muttering under his breath and followed closely by Whistler who was screeching, "Where the hell were you? I combed all the cellblocks and where were you? Relaxing in the goddamned can!"

Dan made a mental note to reward the hapless fellow with a few passes to leave his cell in the evenings. Still convinced that Topper, if not actively involved, had been aware of this plot, Dan decided that this was his chance to flush him out.

Inclement weather began and continued through the holidays. Dan realized this would be instrumental in a cancellation of the planned escape and the few who were involved would be watching the skies nervously until the warden announced that "The annual Santa Claus sleigh ride through the compound distributing candy and fruit to the children will be cancelled this year due to bad weather. We hope to continue this tradition next year."

When Dan arrived at his office on the following morning, there was a Christmas card propped on his desk and he smiled as he read,

"Merry Christmas! Never fear! Santa will return next year!"

Chapter IX

A sudden icy draft of air scouring the café heralded the arrival of a customer swooshing across the threshold. Herbert Angel breezed in with a flurry of soapy fragrances that battled the fish odors. After whisking the bowler from his head and twirling it through the air in an arc toward the hat rack with practiced precision, he bounced over to Dan's table. Time had eroded the blemishes and bruises that develop between men in opposite corners of the ring, leaving a clear sense of respect for one another.

As Louie brought Dan's clam chowder, Angel rubbed his chilled hands together and said, "I'll have the same."

"Do you want dinner or just the chowder?"

"Why I'll have the dinner of course. I could smell that chicken on the ferry, Charley." Reaching for a basket of crackers and buttering one, Angel heaved a sigh, loudly proclaiming, "This place is creaking worse than my old bones."

Perched over the water's edge on pilings, the little café groaned and whined with each wave of the incoming tide.

Dan, with a mouthful of hot chowder, could only nod in agreement while watching Ham Crane's approach.

Seeing Dan's stare, Angel looked back over his shoulder, "Howdy Charley, you still here? Don't you ever go home?"

"This is my home." Crane said, sweeping his arm in a wide arc while he leaned toward Dan. "Hear you've been agitating for changes up there," he said, gesturing toward the prison.

With a hint of annoyance in his voice, Dan looked at Crane and said, "I haven't been agitating for anything."

"Then I've heard wrong." Sniffing loudly, Ham Crane said and looked over at Angel who was frowning as he said, "Better check your artery, it must have a kink in it."

Ignoring the remark, Crane turned to leave, saying,"I also heard those sweeping changes include you, Dan."

Waiting for a response that never came, Crane clutched the ivory head of the cane and limped over to the checkers game in the corner.

Watching the retreating figure, Angel's face puckered as he said, "Never trusted that man. Heard he was raised up the country in some orphanage called Saint Lukes, and those people are really different, if you ask me. In a strange way, I can understand. The cold halls of an orphanage are a poor substitute for a mother's arms, or the crack of a horsewhip for a father's voice."

Memories triggered by Angel's words haunted Dan that night as he returned to a cottage in 1916 Ireland through that magical trigger in the brain that releases pictures from the past.

The woman in the bed was dying and as Dan bent over to clasp her limp hand, she sighed as if signaling a greeting. He placed a cold cloth on her fevered face and cracked lips, whispering, "It's the music, ma, can you hear it? The pipes! They're playing for you."

She stirred and weakly attempted to raise her head, then squeezed his hand.

Through the night he had remained by the bed unable to rise from the chair and release her hand as if that very movement would release her soul. He must have dozed because as dawn crept through the cloud-strewn sky, pushing a faint hint of light through the window, he was jarred awake. The fire had died out in the stove and the chill in the room was as cold as the hand he still clasped. Sometime during the night she had died, waiting until he slept to avoid a final farewell. For long moments Dan remained staring into her worn face; then rose, folded the hands across her breast, brushed the hair matted with perspiration, sprinkled holy water on her lips and said a short prayer.

Death had arrived with a whimper instead of the great shout of a Bach overture accented by fiddles and haunting bagpipes escorting the soul from its earthly ties, he thought as he walked through the door and toward the church in search of a priest.

The damp morning air stung his lungs as he breathed deeply, trying to push away the memories of that house where her body now reposed. The horse whippings that invaded his dreams were dim memories since he had fled years before to apprentice with Seamus O'Flarity, the county veterinarian. Yet, upon the news of his mother's illness, Dan had summoned the courage to return one last time. Walking through the door had been very difficult even with the knowledge that the old man had died in a drunken stupor several years before. Somewhere he was sure there would be a small boy crouched in a closet, cringing with fear and he opened each closet door before entering the small bedroom in the rear of the cottage.

After he had fled the beatings, Dan continued sending money to his mother which she never acknowledged until he later learned that she had donated all of it to the church.

"She never blamed you, Danny," Father O'Mahoney was saying as they stood on the steps of the old church. "She was proud of your accomplishments and always said that you were a fine son. And I believe it was the guilt that made her reject your money. To her, it was tainted with bad memories."

"And what did she say of him?"

"I know," the priest sighed. "She refused to condemn that sadistic man which I will never understand. Perhaps it's called the sin of omission that act of allowing the cruel beatings to continue."

"And you, Father? You knew about it. So what was your excuse?"

For long moments the men faced one another and the old priest's eyes filled with tears as he quickly looked away from the searching eyes of the younger man. Reaching for a cigarette with trembling hands and evading the question with his usual habit of always responding to any statement with a question of his own, he said, "Well, it's back you are now, Danny. What will you do?"

"I'm only here to bury her." Dan said as he gazed into the far mountain peaks bandaged in billowing clouds, "and then I'm off to a war."

At the cemetery where the body, encased in a pine box, was lowered into the grave, Dan said farewell to his past.

Because he was feeling slightly jubilant in his ability to thwart an escape plan that could have presented a danger to the guards as well as their families, Dan decided to push ahead for his sports program by going to the legislature. First, he decided to meet with the parole board to avoid any future confrontations.

"The board has consisted of two prominent men from the community," Jake said one day when they were at the rifle range for a required target practice. "Along with the warden, his aide and a governor's appointee, there's usually a relative or a heavy campaign contributor. That's about it," he turned away, sighting his gun and staring down the field.

"I'm curious," Dan was holding a rifle, looking across at the target range near the cemetery where a guard was adjusting targets. "How are they appointed?"

"The board? They've always been a diversified group from the beginning years of the prison, changing with each administration and trying to appease people who are forced to live alongside a fortress filled with criminals. That's about all I know, Dan," Jake was removing his gloves and wiping his rifle. Then, lighting a cigarette and tossing the match into a sand-filled bucket, he frowned, looking off into the distance. "It's a problem because as the prison population grows so do local tensions. The fear of a successful escape attempt that could involve taking citizens as hostages, hangs over the board like a refrain from the score of a *Bela Lugosi* horror movie."

A dairy rancher who claimed to be a distant descendant of a Portuguese king, owned hundreds of acres adjoining the prison and was a loud dissident when any suggestion was proposed for purchasing property to expand the prison grounds, arose at a board meeting.

"Cardoza, it would help the situation here if you parted with a few acres to improve the strangulation problem now occurring," Rogers had suggested at a recent meeting.

"Get another goddamned prison, then!" Cardoza shouted. "And let 'em strangle one another, good riddance! My roots have been here longer than this goddamned prison!"

The governor was fully aware he could force the sale but was wise enough to realize the consequences in living beside an enemy who would constantly harass, at considerable expense to the state, so he continued to appease the rancher.

"Oh, shit," Rogers once exclaimed. "Eventually the state will get the land but not in my time, that's for sure."

Having met one or two board members on different occasions, Dan felt that this rancher, the most vehement opponent of the prison, was also a fair-minded man. Once again, trusting in his ability to judge human nature, it was to Ferdinand Cardoza that Dan cast his appeal at the meeting one morning in May.

Rogers and Whistler, with his notepad, settled into the chairs along the edge of the gleaming dining room table in the warden's home and patiently waited for the members of the board to arrive. The meeting was set for ten in the morning but some would be arriving on the ferry in Sausalito and Rogers had arranged for a staff car to transport them to the prison. The first member to enter the room was the rancher, Ferdinand Cardoza, who, in his usual brusque manner, simply nodded as he pulled over a chair. "What's on the agenda today? I have to leave in an hour, so let's get on with it."

"Soon as the others get here," Rogers said in a low voice with no audible irritation.

"Well, before the others get here, let me meet this Loot person." Cardoza was lighting a cigar as he spoke, smoke swirling, twisting and outlining each word with a puff.

Whistler and Rogers glanced at one another. "Well, what have you heard?"

"I've heard nothing," Cardoza said, looking sharply at Rogers. "I just had a letter from him, that's all."

91

"A letter?" Whistler was noticeably agitated.

Observing Whistler keenly, the man blowing smoke in his direction, added, "That's what I said. You need a hearing aid, sir?"

Whistler's face reddened, "He sent you a letter about what?"

"Oh," Cardoza said as he reached into his coat pocket and pulled out some papers. "Let's see, he's asking what I thought of sports in this dump."

"Really?" Rogers was growing angry, "And what did you tell him, sir?"

"I haven't seen him yet. I told him to be at this meeting, that's all." He leaned back in the chair, puffing on the cigar while studying the two men. "However, after making some inquiries, I learned that he was able to single-handedly break-up an attempted escape plot over the holidays, is that true?"

"Where did you hear that? That's absolutely not true!"

Cardoza looked over at Whistle, saying, "Is that so? I'll have to double-check my sources."

"Well," Rogers said, coughing, "he did deduce some strange happenings and thought it might be an escape plot but the weather foiled any plans, if there were any. We were never sure, you know."

"Oh. Well, I'd like to meet him anyway."

"Certainly," Rogers leaned back. "Soon as the others get here, I'll send for him."

"No need to," Cardoza said, smiling. "I already contacted his office and asked him to be here by ten."

A worried frown creased Rogers' forehead and he glanced across at Whistler who was busily taking notes.

Ferdinand Cardoza, a large man with regal bearing who enjoyed flaunting his wealth and power, wore an enormous diamond ring on his pinkie finger that flashed in the sunlight as he flicked cigar ashes into a large ceramic ashtray on the table. This strangely annoyed Rogers who angrily lit a cigarette, deliberately flicking the ashes on the thick red rug under his feet.

The room had been decorated by a prior warden's wife, with furniture upholstered in red from the heavy velvet drapes and chair cushions to the embossed wallpaper along one wall depicting colonial scenes. Bright brass buttons on the cushions and pillows glittered as patterns of sunlight sifted through the tall glass windows that opened to a screened porch sheathing the entire south side of the home.

The aged Victorian home assumed an imperious position on a hill overlooking the bay, sitting in detached silence and shunning the prison like an unsavory relative.

Accompanied by a guard, the two remaining members of the board arrived just as Dan entered through the veranda with Sawbucks and Jake.

The building contractor, Art Shaw, a burly man with long white sideburns, resembled an educator yet spoke in the rough vernacular of the stevedore he had once been before entering the construction business. The other board member, Herman Gold, was a mild-sounding man with a soft smile, thinning hair, questioning eyes and a nervous habit of repeating each question. This appointment came through his mother, the governor's sister. No one was sure exactly what he did other than live at home.

After Roger's introduction, the members took seats while Dan stood near Rogers, with Sawbucks and Jake remaining by the glass doors, lending moral support.

Glancing at the papers on the table, Rogers said, "We're here to decide on punishment procedures used here, solitary confinement to be exact................"

"Wait one minute, sir," Cardoza interrupted. "I had asked for the Loot's presence here first, so let's proceed with that." Turning to the other members, he said, "The Loot has something to say, so let's hear it."

They nodded in agreement, settling back in the chairs as Dan began to speak. "Well, this will be brief. First, I'd like to thank Mr. Cardoza who was kind enough to hear me on the subject of sports for the prisoners."

A loud groan erupted from Shaw. "What the hell? That's a crappy idea and how the shit did he ever get in this room?"

Cardoza rose, saying, "Hold it Shaw! I asked him, so let's hear him out!"

Dan, looking uncomfortable, paused for breath. "As I was saying, my idea for sports is well-founded in prison systems in other parts of the world. If you don't want constant riots in the yard, food strikes in the mess hall and knifings in the cellblocks, you have to keep these men occupied in something other than the jute mill, laundry and shops. You, as board members should know what happens on weekends in those cells where the men are caged so densely that nerves erupt on the least provocation. Now, my idea is simple. A few paraphernalia along with some necessary sports equipment, some of which I have collected or been promised by people such as gym managers and team coaches is all I'm asking for, as well as permission to hold games inside, and the space to hold them. I'll take care of the rest. And here," he added, waving papers before setting them down on the table. "I have signed promises from important and responsible people willing to help in the future with donated items and I have even one team in the city volunteering to come inside the prison and play baseball if we had a field." Dan placed the papers on the table and stood back.

In the silence, a ticking clock on the wall sent messages every second while from the rear of the house, the clatter of dishes and aroma of a luncheon being prepared perfumed the air.

"Are there any questions?" Dan looked around hopefully. "Jake and Sawbucks are also here to help with any question."

After a few minutes passed, Rogers rose and said, "Okay, Dan, you men can go. We'll get back to you."

Dan walked around the table, shaking hands with the astonished board members who still hadn't uttered a word. As he walked through the screen porch and down the steps, Sawbucks said, "Shit! Dan! They didn't hear a word, did they?"

"It's hard to say. What do you think, Jake?"

"My thoughts, Dan, you were bucking hard time in there. Those jerks have no idea what a cellblock looks like, let alone imagine a weekend spent locked in one."

"Maybe," Dan said and then stopped and looked back up the hill, "we should arrange a walk through some weekend, what do you think?"

"It couldn't hurt. Do you believe Rogers and Whistler will agree to that?"

"No."

The formal letter on prison stationery, arrived the following day, signed by Whistler. "As secretary of the prison board, it is my duty to inform you that your request for a sports program inside the prison has been denied."

The shades of night had dropped a final curtain across the earth as footlights slowly blinked out in the yard when Dan walked from his office and joined Angel waiting by the front gate, on their way to Witt's End.

"Now I know how a con feels when he's turned down by the parole board." Dan was lamenting as Angel shook his head, "True, but you don't have to return to that dark cell, either."

"What makes you think not?" Glancing around at the gray stone walls that had him handcuffed in their cold stare, Dan shivered.

"Strange, isn't it that the one board member interested in hearing your pitch is the negative one."

"Yeah, and as long as Rogers and Whistler have a vote, I'll never win."

"Maybe there are other ways." Angel looked hopeful.

"Oh sure, there's the rub. I can't jeopardize my job."

At Witt's End that evening, they shared a meal in quiet thought, gazing across the waters at the bright city lights which Informer had once described in an editorial, "To us, the peanut gallery of life, those lights are merely flags at half-mast in the graveyard of the night."

Chapter X

Informer, the newspaper editor and world cynic, was waiting on the Porch when Dan arrived for work.

"Informer is a walking question mark," Jake laughingly remarked, "Even looks like one!"

Dan watched Informer strolling across the room toward his desk, leaning into the breeze, head bent, with muscles quivering like so many electrical impulses humming along a telephone wire.

"Hey, Loot!" His jovial greetings hid a bitter soul, Dan thought, as he exchanged greetings in his usual snappish manner, "Okay, what is it now?"

"Aw, Loot, you sound unhappy. Turned down again, huh?"

"What is it you want?" Impatience seeped through his voice, spiking each word, and Informer stopped smiling.

"Sorry, Loot. Know what this means to you. Always thought you were really smart but you sure weren't thinking when you went before the board without the permission and blessing of the Magi."

Dan, clearly agitated by now, took another look at the long line of fish waiting on the Porch to be processed and, inhaling his cigarette deeply, silently counted to ten then calmly asked, "So, why are you here?"

"Ah, actually I was here to get a report on the progress you're making in the pursuit of a playground for the boys here, sir. When will the slides and swing sets arrive?"

Dan almost burst into laughter as he tried to control himself, tossing the lit cigarette into an ashtray and turning away. Sawbucks also smothered a laugh behind the newspaper he was reading.

"All right, Informer, I have no idea when my sports program will be approved and you can print that."

"Thank you, sir."

"You're welcome. Need anything else before I go to work?"

"Looks like opening day at the trout derby, sir. Reeling in any big fish today?" Informer nodded toward the line of men patiently waiting along the Porch.

"No. It's just our usual run-of-the-mill crappies, sharks, barracuda's and cut-throats."

"Great! Sir! You've really gotten good at this job."

"Consider that a compliment from you, Informer."

The two men stood silently appraising one another for a few minutes then Informer turned away but not before giving a thumbs-up signal to the office staff.

"Hey, Dan," Sawbucks looked puzzled. "What the hell did he mean by that?"

"Who knows what anything means in this place!"

Watching Informer walk along the Porch, Sawbucks turned around in his chair, "You know, there's a man in a hurry, rushing into the next minute!"

"No sympathy for him," Dan reminisced as Sawbucks joined him for coffee at his desk. "He has more talent in one finger than most of the men in here have in their entire bodies. And you know what he suffers from other than inflated ego, too damned much pride!"

Sawbucks nodded. "Prison's full of that!"

"But it's interesting that Informer doesn't recognize that fact."

"Maybe he does, Dan. He refuses to see himself as anything but a genius packed away by a green-eyed society."

Reflecting on their conversation, both men watched the subject of their discussion standing on the Porch lighting a cigarette, taut as a coiled rattlesnake ready to strike at any target offering news. *One could almost visualize a tall peppery Cagney-like character,* Dan thought, *hat at a rakish angle, elastic bands restraining shirt sleeves from dipping into ink wells as he wrote scathing editorials.* Searching and sniffing, Informer was the inveterate newsman who refused to let prison bars hinder him in his search for truth, rumor or gossip.

"So, when does the dance begin?" Informer had returned and was slouched along the railing separating the office staff from the officers' desks, pen and pad in hand.

"Ah," Sawbucks said, grinning, "bad news. It's been postponed indefinitely, Informer. Replacing the gallows will take some time."

Dan continued reading the prison newspaper, ignoring the question as Sawbucks laughed at the reference to the gallows Informer once called the *floorless jig.*

"You know you shouldn't write such drivel."

"What? What the hell did I write that was so bad?"

"This story is about last month's execution." Dan began to read aloud: "Another case of a diseased and frenzied mind has been x-rayed, treated and cured on Wash Day." Leaning back in his chair, Dan looked at the prisoner who, with raised eyebrows, feigned surprise saying, "Aw hell, Loot, it's the truth. That creep lived too long with all his appeals. Besides, I didn't report all the messy details of his execution."

"Stories like this raise hell on the outside. And most people don't know that *Wash Day* refers to an execution. They'll think you were discussing our laundry practices."

Dan ignored Informer's last remark because he had been trying to forget that day when the prisoner struggled to escape from the guards taking him into the gallows. With his brute strength breaking the wrist restraints, he had raced naked around the room while shocked witnesses fled through the doors until armed guards arrived, shackling him, screaming and cursing,

"Goddamn you, God! You old sonofabitch! Where in the shit are you, anyway? You know that I'm not guilty!"

Soon, with the help of a sedative administered by the prison doctor and the calming prayers of the chaplain, the prisoner meekly walked across the stage where a hood was placed over his head and with the aid of two burly guards, he went quietly to his death.

"Some just don't cooperate nicely," one guard remarked to the shocked witnesses who were still shaking from the distressing sight.

"In this stone-coated palaestra, we, the peanut gallery of life, are tested and found wanting. That freedom we once cast away like an old lover now looms above like a pot of gold at the end of a distant rainbow. From the window of our cells at night we see city lights beckoning from across a shark-infested bay, teasing and advertising a world we once scorned. In our loneliness, we cry."

Informer's writing always became nostalgic, moody and melancholy, before his scheduled appearance before the parole board, as if sensing that he would be denied parole but hoping the members would consider his sensitive nature. Today, he decided to appear less cocky and more repentant before the board.

"Loot, it's so damned hard to be repentant when that death was a goddamned accident, for Chrissakes! It's not like I went to a saloon with murder on my mind."

"My guess is that they have a hard time believing you when you're strutting before them tossing quotes from Milton, Darwin, Freud and a former Chief Justice of the Supreme Court. Also, you went to the saloon with boozing on your mind."

"You're saying that they resent my intelligence."

"No, I'm saying they probably take umbrage at the fact that you think you're smarter than them. People don't like loud-mouth braggarts!"

"Thanks for the tip. I'll be a very meek beggar, er, bragger, sir!"

"Also, remember that with all your education and their apparent lack of it, you're the one behind bars."

In the office a week later, Sawbucks turned from the paper he was reading, saying, "Hey, Dan. Did you know Informer was turned down again?"

"So I heard. But this time his return engagement will be in a year not the usual four years."

"And that means?"

"We've got to find a replacement. This paper is important not only to the inmates but also to the guards."

Sawbucks laughed, saying, "Yeah, probably their only reading material."

"The cons?"

"No. I mean the guards. We all love the gossip he throws in from time to time."

Dan paused on his walk across the prison grounds from his home to ingest the seascape on this warm spring morning. The bay was still as a hanging tapestry painted deep blue by the sky as several sailboats floating above the water were sketched stark white against the cobalt canvas. *There were times when the vast beauty of the area needed to be inhaled before tackling the brassy world of the prison*, he thought.

"Dan." Jake's voice on the phone was shrill. "The board is making noises about investigating the Stones and since Rogers and Whistler are away at the capitol today, I'm in charge." He chuckled for a moment, then said, "Since Rogers has stubbornly refused to change things, I think while he's away, we can make some changes before the board makes their planned tour of the area."

"Changes to be made without his approval?"

"Well, why not? What the hell can he do? Yell that we cleaned up the place against his wishes? I don't think so."

"Okay, I'll get right to it."

"Thanks, Dan. You don't have to take anyone with you. Just go on down there and see what's happening. The last time I was there, a few of the boys were being held an unusually long time but there wasn't much I could do about it since it's not my territory. Oh, and report back to me when you've finished your tour."

Walking through a section of the prison that had not been on his watch bothered Dan who felt he was stepping on some unfriendly toes, but it was an order. The Stones actually was a dungeon but someone in another time suggested that it was an eerie place of sorrow and therefore silent as a stone. Although it has often been suggested that at one time men were brought there to be physically stoned to death, that fact was never mentioned in any history of the prison. Nevertheless, that rumor still persisted into the Twentieth Century.

Located in the basement of an aged building that housed the tailor shop, shoe shop, and laundry, the very depth of the room suggested the bottom of the sea. It reeked with the dank odors of mold and mildew, only lacking the tendrils of swirling, floating algae, sea moss and kelp. The dampness penetrated bones, invaded lungs and chilled the skin, making movement of any kind painful. If there had been windows, one would expect to look out into a world of exotic fish swimming around the hulls of sunken ships with divers in colorful gear searching for hidden treasures while fighting off sharks. But there were no windows here just as there were no doors, carpeted rooms, warmth or song, only the humming of an insane man off in a corner cell and the stomping of the many washing machines on the floor above, testifying to life.

Walking down the stairs, Dan shivered, not from the dampness but from a faded memory. A guard posted at the bottom of the staircase leading to a row of cells, saluted as Dan approached. "Hi, Loot, time you came to see how the other half lives. Welcome to Goofy Alley."

"What's your name?" Dan asked, finding the humor tasteless.

"Jack Daws, sir. Cons call me Flapjack."

After motioning for a key, Dan walked past the dark cells which were narrow cubicles, barely wide enough for one man to squat inside, containing a slop bucket and mattress on the stone floor. These were reserved for the hard-core criminals and those judged insane by the prison doctor and needing only one prison official attesting to that fact.

Peering into a cell, Dan saw only blackness but the putrid odors from its mouth were stifling and he quickly backed away.

"I wouldn't open that, sir."

Ignoring the guard, Dan opened the cage door and looked inside. "Okay, come on out"

As the prisoner crept through the yawning black hole, hands raised to protect eyes blinded by light, Dan saw a shriveled bag of rags attempting to stand upright but too weak to remain there. Slipping to the ground, the prisoner smiled self-consciously and said, "Sure look silly, sir," and weakly squatted back on his heels.

Jesus! This is the 1930s! Are we still in the Dark Ages? Dan thought as he drew out a package of cigarettes from his pocket, offering one to the dumb-struck prisoner who eagerly accepted the light as Dan bent over to light it.

"I thank you, sir, whoever you are." His voice was shaky yet carried a note of dignity. As he spoke, Dan remembered that a few weeks ago when Informer had mentioned a defiant prisoner too long in the Stones.

"He wouldn't divulge some information about concealed weapons inside, sir."

"Don't expect me to help if he won't cooperate, Informer."

Informer had walked away dejectedly, saying, "Of all the guards here, you were the one I thought would help him. He's really an intelligent guy who's too loyal to the wrong people!"

"That's not a trait of an intelligent man, Informer."

"In here it is, sir."

Today, Dan was attempting to hide his shock at the sight of this emaciated, bearded skeleton with swollen hands and empty eyes.

"How long has he been in here?" Dan asked the guard who was staring open-mouthed, saying, "Damned if I know. Just shove in the food and water and don't ask questions."

"That seems to be the standard answer these days. Well, get on the phone and send for a stretcher."

The guard hesitated, a questioning look on his flat face.

"Go!" Dan snapped, "I'll take responsibility. I want this man in the hospital now."

"Aw shit, not the hospital. Just let me die here and not there," the prisoner said.

"You're not dying and you won't die there, either."

While they waited for the stretcher, his lifeless eyes stared into space and the prisoner began to speak in a stronger voice, "Still alive, sir."

Dan nodded as his eyes scanned the remaining cells.

The meeting with Rogers and Jake occurred on the following day at Dan's request after leaving the Stones.

"Shit, Dan, those Stones have been there forever. Only used in severe cases, you know."

"Have you been down there lately?"

"No," Rogers replied sharply as he studied Dan, "I leave that to Whistler."

For a while, both men faced off and it was as if each read the other's mind and didn't like what he read.

Leaning back in the chair and swiveling around to gaze across the prison, Rogers laughed. "What are you proposing, getting rid of dungeons and replacing them with playing cards?" Sarcasm was dripping with each pinched word as the warden studied the landscape through the heavy smoke of his cigar.

"No, I just want you to go over there and then make some changes."

"What changes?"

"Maybe you'll have some ideas, sir, after you see the situation."

Rogers sighed deeply, pushed a button on the desk and Whistler appeared in the doorway, pen and pad in hand.

"Make an appointment for my visit to the Stones tomorrow."

Whistler raised his eyebrows, asking, "Why?"

"Never mind why, just do it!"

Glancing at his pad, Whistler was nodding as he spoke, "However, you have a meeting in the city tomorrow. What about next week?"

Dan and Jake walked out in disgust, knowing this would give Whistler time to secure the place and perhaps move the worst cases.

"Well, in that case, at least the place will be cleaned and we've done some good." Jake said, scowling as he walked toward the front office. "I don't think that the board will bother coming in, anyway. Do you?"

"From the little I saw of them, they only seem to come here for that free lunch!"

"Ah, you're just bitter, Dan," Jake joked as they parted.

On the chance that Whistler decided to scour the area before the warden's inspection, Dan walked over to the Stones on the following morning. Nothing appeared to have changed. Pleading voices were still calling to a deaf world and the putrid odors still warped the air like a unique perfume from hell. However the flat-faced guard was not there, to Dan's surprise.

"Where's Flapjack?"

The startled guard dropped his sandwich and said, "Don't know. Just was called from the barracks this morning so I didn't have time for breakfast, sir."

Dan waved his hand, saying, "That's all right. Go ahead and eat. Have any of these men been moved today?" He was gesturing toward the dark cells.

"No. Wish they'd stop whining."

"Okay, open all the cells now."

"All of them, now, at once, sir?"

"That's what I said, open all the cells. Just walk down the row and open sesame!" Dan said, impatiently snapping his fingers.

Jake walked in at this point. "Going ahead with this, Dan?"

"Yeah. Do you agree?"

"I'm behind you," Jake said as the guard saluted Jake, saying, "Morning sir."

Jake sniffed and said, "Lousy duty here."

After slowly opening the cell doors, the guard noticed that no one stirred but the voices had ceased calling. All was silent once again in the Stones.

At this moment the jute mill whistle blew and in the distance a train sending its hoarse trill from the edge of the bay, harmonized. Dan walked along the row, bending and ordering each occupant out. Gradually, six faces blinked through the iron doors, some with dazed, empty looks, some stone-faced and others with belligerent stares, including a stream of saliva. As they crawled slowly toward the brick wall where Dan stood, they heard his orders for six stretchers and watched a startled guard reach for the telephone.

Later, back in his office, Dan ordered a cleaning crew sent to the Stones, shouting into the phone, "I wouldn't put a sewer rat in those cages!"

The shouted response carried over the wires was heard throughout the office, "That's who IS there!"

Sawbucks leaned back in his swivel chair, hands clasped behind his head, watching Dan. "You saw the Stones and you're shocked? Hell, Dan, you should have seen it before Rogers became warden. He did a lot to sanitize this joint."

"Maybe he did but there sure as hell is still a lot to do!"

Of the six men released from the Stones, two were found to be totally incompetent by a team of doctors brought in and were consequently sent to a hospital for the insane in the southern part of the state.

Informer wrote in his newspaper editorial, "The need for a hospital for insane criminals is long overdue."

The others were released to return to their former cells after Jake appeared before Rogers and the board, stating, "These men were sent in there for life. Their crimes were withholding information about illegal activities here. I think they've served enough time and should return to their old cell blocks."

It was agreed upon by all the members of the board who signed a document to reassign the men to cellblocks.

Rogers beamed when he received a letter of commendation for his exposure on the conditions in the Stones, resulting in a cleaner environment for the incarcerated felons.

"It wasn't hard to see that those conditions could not be tolerated in modern times," Rogers said as he read the letter to the staff meeting.

"Never mentioned us, Dan," Jake commented as they walked from the building after the meeting.

"Did you expect him to?"

"No, guess not."

"Well, they're not tearing down the place until some money is allotted by the state but at least they'll be in clean cells until then."

"Don't want to make it too nice for them," Jake said, frowning.

"No, they're in here to be punished which doesn't mean floggings and starvation."

"Yep. It's been proposed to rip the place down and build a new set of cells that'll segregate the younger prisoners from the hard-timers."

"Finally, the board is joining the Twentieth Century!"

When Dan inquired about the prisoner who had been too long in the Stones, he saw a youth with scraggly blonde hair and beard accompanied by a belligerent attitude, shackled to a bed in the hospital wing.

"I've killed all my life and if you release me, you're giving me a chance to kill you and I guarantee you that I will."

Dan, remembering his own rebellious youth fostered by a sadistic father, recognized the anger but also detected the familiar lone note of forlornness.

"Belligerency will get you nowhere here so why don't you consider an opportunity I'm about to offer."

"What?" A sudden glint in eyes otherwise shaded by an awning of suspicion, clued Dan he was on the right track.

"I need someone with your knowledge of punishment and how you survived that long in the Stones. You could be a liaison between my office and the men."

"What would I do?"

"Indoctrinate them by relating your experiences and the futility of defiance."

"What's in it for me?"

"Other than a life in solitary confinement? Well, a comfortable cell in the trusties' section, good meals and a chance at an education in the school here."

"You're offering me a job as trustee?"

"Yes."

The prisoner laughed. "Me? You know the first minute I can, I'll escape and kill, maybe you."

"I'll take that chance."

"And stoolie? No fucking way!" He turned his face toward the wall. Rising from the chair, Dan started for the door. "Well, consider my offer. It expires at midnight," he said and walked away without looking back.

"You're offering that con a trustee's job? He's one of the most notorious rebels in here! In the past he's been responsible for riots and is suspected of smuggling weapons inside!" Sawbucks was livid as he reached for his cap, saying, "I won't be a part of this, Dan!"

"Don't blame you and I don't expect your help but I know what I'm doing. Right now, he's their martyr. They expect him to go back to the Stones. When that happens, who knows what they'll do. I can feel the tension whenever I walk through those goddamned cellblocks."

Later that day when Dan returned to the office, Sawbucks was standing by his desk and, replacing the phone, said, "The hospital called and Croaker says that con you dragged down from the Stones the other day, wants to talk to you."

"What does he want to talk about?"

"About what the hell the word *indoctrinate* means!"

Dan laughed as he picked up the phone and called the hospital.

"Release him?" Croaker was indignant, saying, "Never! This man is a killer!"

"You're right, so send him over to my office now and without those goddamned shackles!"

107

"This is your responsibility and I want it in writing before I release him!"

"Consider it done." Dan calmly replaced the phone and waited for all hell to break loose. However, hell would have to wait.

Chapter XI

After the escape plot that had been thwarted by the inclement weather last year, there was always the stressful anticipation of a repeat performance as each holiday season approached. When the jute mill whistle shrieked this morning, a shiver ran through Dan's body and a realization that this was the wrong time of day for that whistle, as well as the wrong season!

Today, as a warm breeze playfully slapped the flag against its pole, a short prisoner, hair flying in the wind and screaming, was seen fleeing along the path from the warden's home, frantically waving a white apron over his head like a flag of truce.

"Fire, fire!" the Chinese cook was yelling as two guards, rushing from the front office, raced across the street toward him.

Excitedly pointing toward the warden's mansion, the man kept screaming, "Fire, fire!" At this point other guards had gathered, including Sawbones, who quickly realized the seriousness of the man's fear.

"There seems to be trouble up there." Sawbones nodded toward the house on the hill incubating in the lush green foliage of pomegranate trees and enormous oleander shrubs.

"No smoke coming out," another guard commented as they formed a small knot of men around the frightened prisoner.

"A board meeting's going on in there today," Dan said, breathless as he arrived after racing through the yard. "Rogers and Jake are also in there with the board."

"Oh, hell!" Sawbucks saw the situation. "There's an escape attempt going on right now in that house with our men trapped inside!"

"It's an escape, sir? Should we get weapons?" A young guard looked puzzled, wondering if this was the great escape that had been the topic of discussion over coffee ever since that scare at Christmas.

"Yes." Dan looked over at the armory which was already open as men filed across the bridge into the building. The shaking prisoner was still jabbering, "Robbers, robbers,"

"Is he saying robbers, sir?" The guard looked again at Dan who nodded. "Okay, take this little guy inside and call for an immediate lockdown and head count!"

"Lockdown and head count in progress, Dan," Sawbucks exclaimed, pressing past the confused guard as he took the prisoner by the arm. "You can take him inside and then join us, okay?" The guard was so relieved to be assigned a duty that he eagerly grabbed the protesting inmate who kept hollering, "I do nothing!"

In the large gardens that surrounded the warden's home, several armed guards who had quickly been posted in the orchard whose fruit trees skirted the edge of the property to the east, greeted Dan as they stood surveying the scene with binoculars.

"There's three cons inside," one man said. "I think that's all."

"We'll know after the head count."

As Sawbucks joined them, Dan asked, "Who's in there besides Rogers and Jake?"

"Not sure, but if there's a board meeting, that would bring the number to three, four, or more, if Whistler is also there."

"Whistler's off today, sir," a guard volunteered.

"Okay, then that means there are five men in there with the three cons, right?" Sawbucks looked at Dan who turned binoculars on the house and asked, "Weapons?"

"Well from what I could see, one has Rogers' revolver and another con has what looks like a fake weapon of some kind."

"How did they get in?"

"Delivering some flower arrangements, the Chinaman said."

"Who let them in?"

"Don't know. The cook's English isn't very good."

The gardens surrounding the Victorian home were the pride of the prisoners who had turned the small knoll into a spectacular setting of color for the white home with a wrap-around veranda. Jasmine, honeysuckle and bougainvillea straddled the porch pillars and crawled along the roof. The heady essence of flowering shrubs coated the air while geraniums fled down the hillside chased by ivy that crept between the hedges.

The small group that gathered by the house were an elite group selected for their sharp-shooting ability demonstrated at the rifle range and on occasion inside the prison yard. In a tense situation, some were known to have picked-off a weapon in the hands of a threatening prisoner from a distant tower, without injury. Now alert, they awaited orders while the warden, captain and board members were held in the hands of desperate men.

"The story is that the warden's cook admitted the delivery man into the kitchen," Sawbucks said. "Then he herded the kitchen help into a small pantry. Meanwhile, the board members were having lunch, unaware of the situation. The cook was able to crawl through a small window and run for help."

Word quickly reached the men that there were just two prisoners missing but the bad news was that they were among the desperate ones recently released from the Stones.

"These are lifers! Shit! They have nothing to lose by killing because with these charges over their heads, they definitely face the gallows!"

The gravity of the situation was etched on every face as stunned men surveyed the house with trembling hands grasping weapons, knowing the least sound would alert the prisoners to their presence. Dan and Sawbucks were still puzzling over how

111

the men were able to gain entry with a simple ruse of delivering flowers.

"Supposing one of the kitchen help was in on this," Dan said as they continued watching the house. "He might have alerted them when the board was meeting. Otherwise, the cons would never know when those meetings are scheduled."

"Yeah, that's right. They don't set times especially for that reason, I understand."

"But the kitchen help is aware because they have to plan the menus ahead."

"That's right, Dan. I think we have something here."

"Uh, huh. Also, then there are three, not two, cons involved in this. One is in hiding."

"But, who?" Sawbucks asked, puzzled, mentally picturing the kitchen help who were all Chinese. "You know, the Chinese prisoners here don't mix with the others."

"Maybe he isn't Chinese. Maybe he's a gardener who does the flowers for the table. Then again, it could be Topper."

A young guard approached. "Loot, the sheriff just contacted us. Do you need his men?"

"Tell him, thanks, but we think we can handle this. If not, we'll let him know."

"So the word's out in the community. Great!" Sawbucks lit a cigarette with shaking hands, saying, "Topper? Why would you think that?"

Dan shrugged and said, "Just can't get him out of my mind."

"This is entirely all your fault, Dan!" Whistler, wearing his golfing clothes, knickers and plaid cap, was walking toward them, swinging a club. "You had to go down to the Stones and release those animals! I had them just where they should be! If anything happens, I'll have your head!"

Sawbucks looked at the red-faced man. "You know, Whistler, you're making a lot of noise here, so get out before you alert the boys in there and they might come after you too!"

"And you!" said Whistler pointing a finger at Sawbucks. "You'll go with him!"

As they watched him stomp off, a guard asked, "How did he get here? I thought he was on the golf course. Well, I'm supposed to give you this list, Loot."

Dan also wondered about Whistler's presence and filed that thought away.

"Thanks." Dan took the paper, glanced over it and handed it to Sawbucks who whistled. "Whew! Dan! These characters are just one step removed from hell's gate, as far as I'm concerned. This Tommy Holtz, also known as Tom Thumb, was in the Stones because he severely beat another prisoner with an iron pipe. He almost killed him. The poor wretch would've been better dead, severe brain damage."

"What about the other one?"

"Bananas claims to have been a hit man for the Chicago mafia. Killed a security guard at a warehouse and that wasn't his first murder. Both are lifers, Dan."

"I know."

"That means they'll get the full penalty so why not kill Rogers and Jake anyway, just for spite."

"I don't think the board members are any safer."

"Right."

"Hope that Portuguese gent isn't there today. He's so outspoken he would ask for a bullet rather than submit to their demands."

As time slowly passed, the men grew more worried about the safety of the hostages. Just as Dan and Sawbucks were deciding about rushing the house, a guard approached and said, "I got a bead on the one by the window, Loot."

"Where's Rogers?"

"Still at the desk but he's not using the telephone."

"Which means?"

"He's not cooperating."

"I agree," Dan said in a somber voice and asking, "Any ideas, anyone?"

At that moment the most bizarre incident of the entire episode occurred as a slender man, dressed in convict's clothing, burst through the door on the veranda and, crawling across the lawn, screamed, "Don't shoot, don't shoot!" As he rapidly crept toward the guards, he was chased by a man in a brown suit carrying a gun. Upon spying the army of guards, he wheeled around and caught a bullet through his head. For what seemed an eternity, he stood erect with a puzzled expression, the top half of his head blown off, then collapsed into a bloody heap on top of the terrified man who, no longer screaming, had fainted.

Realizing that the next few seconds were crucial, the men rushed the open door just as a shot rang out. Entering the room, they saw Rogers standing over the body of Bananas, gun hanging limply in his hand. Across the room, a convict in a business suit, hands in the air, was pleading, "Don't shoot, don't shoot, they made me do it." He dropped a replica of a gun made from a soap bar. Jake, who by now had freed himself from the ropes that bound his hands, turned and without hesitation, swung at the man, sending him reeling across the room. Then as he turned to the others, the convict's pants he was forced to wear dropped to the floor and Jake stood before the world in boxer shorts covered with Valentine hearts!

"If I hear any smart mouth, I'll send you over to join him on the floor!" Jake yelled as one of the guards hurriedly handed him a jacket.

Their laughter carried across the orchard as the guards returned to the armory with their weapons, humor gilding tense voices with relief.

As the board members gathered in the kitchen, Rogers opened a bottle of Scotch whiskey, saying, "We made it through another crisis, gents. Here's to your health."

Cardoza, the first to complain, said, "I want to know how those men were released from solitaire. Didn't anyone know they were vicious?"

Rogers, looking across at Dan, said, "Indeed! They are the exact reason we need the Stones!"

The board member, after all the bloody gore was cleaned from his head, was brought in from the lawn, weeping and said,

"I never should have accepted this job. Never want to see this hellish place again!"

Dan and Sawbucks began gathering up evidence for the certain trial that would ensue. The gardener, known as the Fixer, confessed to his part in the crime but insisted that he was innocent of any escape plans, saying, "I thought they were just putting a scare into the old man so he'd quit!"

"That's a hard story to swallow when he was the one standing over Rogers with a gun forcing him to call for a car." Sawbucks said, walking through the rooms and checking for any other weapons the men might have brought.

"You know," Dan said, laughing. "I have to credit Rogers. That old man wasn't going to call for any car. I think we all have underestimated him, including the cons."

"Well, I think that crazy Bananas wanted out one way or the other!" Sawbucks said while walking down the slope to the armory with Dan. "What do you think?"

"I don't know." Dan said, reflectively. "I still think Topper was in on this."

"Why would he be?"

"To get rid of Rogers or scare the shit out of him so he'd resign."

"Possible. But hard to prove."

"Someday, I'll ask him."

"Who? Rogers?"

"No. Topper."

Informer had a wonderful time with the story. "The warden, captain of the guard and unnamed board members were stripped naked and robbed at gun point with the warden's gun within the warden's home which is within the prison grounds, surrounded by armed guards. They were not only humiliated but forced to sit at the table dressed in convict's garb! My! What is this world coming to?"

Dan called Informer into his office the following day, saying, "When reporting the news, the most important thing to remember is to report the facts correctly. The warden was not stripped of his clothing and they were not robbed!"

"Oh, shit, Loot! I had to take a goddamned fouled-up escape attempt and make an interesting story. Why can't I just embellish a little? Isn't that called something like poet's license?"

Dan laughed at Informer's deliberate ridicule of a familiar cliché and said, "Probably because your embellishments have gotten you in prison, is one reason. I want a retraction before the whole damned country thinks our prison personnel are total idiots!"

The retraction appeared in the following week's edition:

"We apologize for reporting erroneously that the warden was stripped of his clothes. Actually, he was only stripped of his gun. However, it is true that they were all robbed of their dignity. And our hearts beat for you too, Captain!"

The escape attempt brought the legislature to their feet, demanding stricter laws regarding prison breaks that jeopardized the lives of prison personnel.

A law was soon passed making a death penalty mandatory for anyone serving a life sentence that does bodily harm to a guard or other prisoner. Also, an automatic death penalty was added for anyone committing perjury that results in the execution of another.

Informer's editorial came out on the day the prisoner was handed the death sentence. "Thanks to our late friends, we now have more appendages to the death penalty. Indeed, it was a day in hell when Fixer displayed his usual talent for asininity, sowing his wild oats in the warden's dining room with a gun fashioned from a bar of soap that led him to *Wash Day* for the deaths of his two good buddies. Well done, stupid!"

When the dust had settled after the attempted escape and kidnapping of the warden and board members, Dan was called before the board to explain why those particular criminals were removed from the Stones.

It was a calm autumn day with the air, sullied by burning leaves stinging the eyes as he walked along the hill to the warden's home.

"Just a review of your work here," Shaw stated, "before we get into that incident with the Stones."

They were seated at the same table where the inmates had dined and Dan wondered how uncomfortable it must be for the board members now reduced to the two remaining men, Shaw and Cardoza, who gave no hint of their feelings. Rogers, with Whistler by his side, was seated in the same desk chair he had occupied on that bloody day several weeks before.

"Well, what do you want to know?"

Whistler now spoke up, saying, "If I may, sir, Dan ordered the immediate release of those men to the hospital without any......"

"If I may..." Shaw interrupted, sarcastically, saying, "I was questioning Dan and, besides, I see another signature on this release form."

"Yes, it's mine," Rogers said, uncomfortably shifting in his chair. "In spite of what happened on that day, I still think we did the right thing," he said, glancing towards Dan in a conspiratorial manner.

"But, sir, you went through a trying ordeal and you've even lost a board member because of them." Whistler said, cheeks puffed out in surprise.

Rogers smiled, saying, "I wouldn't call his absence a loss." Pausing in reflection, he looked through the windows toward the bay and turned back to them. "After reviewing your record, Dan, Cardoza and I agreed that you did the right thing at the time since you didn't have foresight. These men were vicious, I grant you that. But even the worst miserable cur in the world must be treated civilly in our society." Leaning back in his chair, he looked again through the window, adding, "Sometimes I think that the harsher men are treated, the meaner they get. Maybe a softer stick, eh?"

"Well, is there anything else we should know about?"

"Yes. What about the Hole?"

They all stared at Whistler who had voiced an unspoken word in the prison.

"What about it?"

"Will we continue to send the most vicious there?"

117

The men glanced at one another, then Cardoza lifting an eyebrow, said, "Why don't we take that up at the next meeting when there is a full forum?"

All agreed, except Whistler, who was very angry, tapping his foot on the carpet repeatedly. "Where will they be punished now? Work has already started on demolishing the Stones, preparing for that new cellblock."

"We'll discuss that at the next meeting, sir." Shaw's voice edged with impatience as he stared at Whistler.

As the men stood and shook hands, Rogers said, "See me before you leave tomorrow, Dan."

Cardoza walked part of the way down the hill with Dan. "I probably should wait but I'm wishing you luck and if you're able to get sports into the prison here, I might consider donating some land for an athletic field. Wait! I didn't promise, I said consider."

"I understand." Dan was smiling and said, "So you agree that sports might alleviate a lot of our problems here."

Shrugging, he said, "I don't know about that but I do know if the men can compete on the field, they'll be losing some of their aggression before they go to the cellblocks."

"My thought exactly, sir."

Dan was still in shock when he returned to the office.

"How'd it go?" Sawbucks had a worried look.

"Oh, it went okay. We're off tomorrow for the capitol, don't forget."

"How could I? This has been dancing around in my head since I first met you."

"If you want to get a sports program started in here, try shooting down the moon with a rubber band. That's how easy it will be." Dan read the unsigned letter, turning it over in his hands as he contemplated its meaning. Tomorrow he was leaving for the capitol with Sawbucks, for the arranged meeting with a senator. Somehow, he sensed this letter came from Topper and he pushed it to the back of the drawer. *This was an interesting turn of events*, he thought. *It's strange that Topper would show his hand now just before my trip to the capitol.*

Smiling, Dan locked the drawer and was walking from the office just as Fetcher crept through the door. "Ah, Loot, sir, can I see you?"

"Will this take long? I'm in a hurry."

"No sir, I never take long with nobody." Chuckling as he scratched his balding head after removing the gray cap, he said, "I been in here so long, Loot, that I rightly forget why."

"Do you want me to tell you why, Fetcher."

"Ah, nossir. Got a feeling it's bad."

"Okay, come on in but I haven't much time for you."

"Oh, I know that, sir, yes sir. You'd be the busiest man in the place here."

Twisting the cap in his hands, he said, "Ah Loot, this parole, let some other guy have it. I ain't got no place to go, sir. This here's my only home since my Sadie died."

"I can't help you, Fetcher and, by God, I wish I could."

Seeing the disappointment on the face of the old man, Dan said, "I already spoke to the warden and his hands are tied. Paroles are out of our hands, you know, it's the parole board's business."

"Yessir," said the old man as he stared at Dan.

"Wait! Didn't the doctor offer you a home?"

"Yessir but I don't want it. This here's my home."

Dan was never sure if the sly old man was putting one over on everyone with his innocent act. As he aged, his duties were limited to running errands and acting as an occasional gate keeper whisking open the front gate for cars entering and leaving the prison grounds. At those times, he would tell anyone within earshot he was looking for a daughter who had disappeared long ago.

"Someday, someday, I'll look up and there she'll be, all dressed in white, like a little angel." He would relate the same story to anyone, including Dan, who encountered him on his rounds.

"Wouldn't it be great if all the cons were like him?" Rogers had said when they had first discussed the old man's parole.

"Wouldn't need any locks or bars, sir," Dan said.

119

"Well, maybe the parole board will have some ideas. He's in for the murder of his wife. Butchered her in the kitchen of their home and threw the body parts into the bay for the sharks. He received a death sentence, later commuted to life with a possibility of parole. The little girl was the prime witness in the trial. Understand she did a disappearing act." Rogers was reading from a probation report on his desk and sighed, shaking his head. "Did you know this was in 1900?"

"Is that so? No, I didn't know. He's been here as long as some of the walls."

"Probably helped build them," Rogers said, laughing.

Today, Dan had a busy schedule, including meeting with Rogers before leaving tomorrow.

"Tell you what, Fetcher, when I get back from my trip tomorrow, we'll call on the good doctor and see what we can do there."

"Thanks Loot but I ain't going to live with him, no way, sir."

The old man was almost comical in appearance as arthritis had shaped his bones in a way that he seemed to be going in all directions at once while shaking his head at some vague remembrance. Dan made a note on his calendar to take Fetcher over to Croaker's office.

Chapter XII

Entering the warden's office that afternoon, Dan was surprised to see that Rogers was alone, reading through some papers while chomping on a cigar.

"Sit, sit." Rogers said, motioning to a chair by his desk without taking his eyes off the paper he was scanning. Then, leaning back in the chair, he studied Dan for a few seconds and said, "You know, and this is just between us, but I think your idea for sports is a good one, Dan."

As he spoke, Dan reached into his pocket for a package of Camels, lit one and snuffed out the match in the ashtray.

"But I can tell you right now, it won't happen as long as this governor is in office."

"Why?"

"I was reading a speech he gave recently to the Rotary Club in the city and in it, I'll quote, he said, "There have been recent murmurings in prison circles that some people are agitating for sports programs for the felons, one put on by criminals inside the prison walls. This is the most ludicrous suggestion I have ever heard in my life! How can one link punishment with play? If a man is sent to prison to be punished for a serious crime and, while there, can enjoy sports in the same way our honest citizens do, isn't that an oxymoron? Why don't we just give them a lollipop and send them to sit in the dunce's corner?"

Dan sat quietly for a few moments in thought, then said, "Is that why you wanted to see me, sir?"

Rogers smiled, saying, "Just thought I'd prepare you for the capitol."

Standing, Dan reached for the uniform cap resting on the desk. "Well, thanks for the warning, sir. I'll remember that when I see the governor."

"Are you seeing him?"

"No, but hope beats eternal, or something like that."

Walking across to his office, Dan saw Informer lounging against a fence, smoking, inquisitive eyes trained on him as he said, "So, hear you're off to tame the lions, sir."

Dan couldn't help smiling at the young man whose humor was always edged with a hint of bitterness.

"If you editorialize my trip, Informer, please spell my name correctly."

"I surely will! Absolutely! I'll capitalize it in fact."

As he turned to walk away, Dan said, "Oh, by the way, if you have room you can note that the Loot took his slingshot with him to Sacramento."

"Whatever that means, sir," Informer saluted, smiling and added, "Will do."

In the next edition of the newspaper, Informer published a tentative list of suggested sports events, asking the men to select their favorites. "Fencing, sharp-shooting, skeet, hammer-throwing, pole-vaulting, as well as the more popular events, swimming and diving are all on the list. And for what it's worth, the Loot asked that I mention the fact that he took his slingshot with him to Sacramento. On second thought, that could also be considered a sport."

Somewhere within the prison compound, laughter echoed across the walls as a man put down the latest edition of the paper and lit a pipe.

An unusual heat wave dropped its glowing embers over the bay and surrounding countryside on the day Dan and Saw-bucks left for the capitol. Even with the breeze from the bay sifting through the windows of the train, Dan felt the perspiration suiting his body and clinging to the shirt as he removed his jacket.

"Unusual for September," Sawbucks said, removing his coat and adding, "Hope this isn't an indication of the hours ahead."

"If you mean, will we be grilled? I hope not."

As the train beat a rapid tattoo on the tracks, Dan leaned back, enjoying the scenery. Swaying, quivering and shaking, they fled over trestles and bridges, rumbled through the patchwork of open fields, opened the back doors of small villages and cautiously hedged the approaches to each town. Then, retracing the tour through the network of streets, whistle blowing, the train fled into a golden-leafed countryside. Slowly creeping into the train depot, brakes squealing, the old iron horse slid to an abrupt stop, tossing those passengers standing by the doors against one another.

Leaving the train, the men walked along a graveled path skirting the tracks, passing the depot, its reddish-brown stain now faded into a faint blush from years of weathering.

Catching sight of a taxi, they hailed it as the driver eyed them suspiciously and said, "First time here?"

"No." Dan said as they settled back into the upholstered seat of the Ford.

"Well, you picked a good day. It's the hottest September on record."

The capitol with a gold dome symbolizing the origin of the state's wealth gleamed in the early morning light as they stepped out into the sultry morning. The cab driver, assuming the role of neighborly ambassador, handed Sawbucks his card, saying, "If you need a little sight-see here in the city, call me."

"What the hell did that mean?" Sawbucks asked, staring at the cab as it disappeared.

"My guess would be that he has a cousin in the rackets," Dan said, laughing. "Or a cousin's daughter available."

Sawbucks reddened, saying, "Jeesus! That's going on right here in the capitol under all their noses."

"Under whose noses?"

"Why, our legislators, you know those guys who make the laws, for Chrissakes!"

Dan laughed, noticing Sawbucks' red face and said, "I think you've been locked away too long!"

"Yeah, you could say I'm a lifer. That's what the wife says."

While walking up the steps, they gaped at the shimmering white capitol building constructed of stone which had taken twenty years to complete. An enormous high-canopied lobby, with spacious wide steps leading to other floors, was of polished marble creating a hollow chamber for footsteps to echo like tap dancers in the hushed building.

At the information booth, a freckled youth clad in a letter sweater from a local college, rang the senator's office and turning to them, waved a hand toward a row of chairs, saying, "If you'll have a seat, he'll be right out."

Sawbucks pulled out a package of cigarettes, offered one to Dan and they sat quietly smoking, watching people rush through the lobby, never noticing them. The wait seemed longer than expected when a tall, deeply-tanned man came striding toward them wearing a big smile and a ten-gallon white straw hat. Dressed in a dark suit, bolo tie, black boots with images of rearing horses and silver spurs that jingled with each step, he seemed to have just jumped off the chuck wagon. An enormous silver belt buckle peered out whenever his jacket swung open and, speaking with a slight western twang, he extended his hand, saying, "Loot? Good to see you. I'm Senator Rafael Corbett and sorry about the delay but that's how it is, these days."

"I've been looking forward to meeting you, Senator Corbett."

"Well, my office is down the hall." He said, glancing at his wrist watch. "And, you know, it's almost noon, so why don't we get a bite to eat in the cafeteria downstairs while we discuss the situation at the prison?"

Thinking that his mission was too important to be discussed in public, Dan smiled and said, "Well, sir, we really aren't hungry," ignoring Sawbucks who was shaking his head vigorously.

"Oh. Then, let's go to my office," he said and veered to the right, walking rapidly along a very dark, cramped hallway to an office at the edge of the building as Dan and Sawbucks trailed, wondering what happened to all the light bulbs in the building.

Opening a squeaking door, he laughed, saying, "Being the newest of the new senators, I was assigned the smallest of the small offices."

The windowless room was paneled with books spilling from the shelves, traveling across the floor and after scaling the walls, settling in disarray on the shelves. A ceiling fan whirred, pushing stale air around while complaining with a series of periodic squeaking.

Dan and Sawbucks had trouble deciding where to sit as the senator swung into his chair. Sawbucks picked an unoccupied shelf to lean against while Dan simply leaned against the door.

"This office explains the reason I had suggested the cafeteria. But, mind you, I'm not complaining. No sir! Not after all the years it took to get here!"

Leaning back in the swivel chair, he lifted his legs, stretching them across the desk as he studied his boots which appeared to be new. "Look at this," he said, moving a leg. "See that boot? The carving of the horse doesn't match the carving on the other boot, does it?"

Dan and Sawbucks leaned over to get a closer look at the expensive boots.

"Looks fine to me," Sawbucks said, peering intently at the boot. Dan nodded in agreement.

"Well, must be the light in here," he said, dropping his legs back on the floor. "Okay, let's get on with this. What's there?" he asked, impatiently pointing to Dan's briefcase.

Quickly retrieving the papers, Dan placed them on the desk, saying, "These are letters of guarantee for athletic gear as well as money and support from many people throughout the city and country. There's also letters from a boxing manager in the city with instructions, the owner of a gymnasium who handles and teaches wrestlers and gymnasts. Also, a private club has offered to send money for future purchases of athletic equipment and a letter from the owner of a well-known baseball club in New York, sir."

Leaning forward, the senator shuffled through the papers, holding some out and pushing others toward Dan.

"Prophesying was never one of my strong points and I wish I could see the future and believe that people do change but I'm inclined to agree with the governor. I guess it's an old cliché - once a con, always a con. Tell me what would happen if these cons decided to take hostages, maybe even a whole baseball team? What would you do? How would you explain it to the citizens of this state?"

Dan stood his ground, saying, "First, these men will always be hand-picked. Most are former athletes and short-timers who know how foolish it would be to do something like you described. Sir, if you ever have a chance to get over there, you'll see the crowded conditions. My argument is that participation in sports with friendly rivalry among themselves or with the outsiders will not only be healthy but reduce aggressive behavior. What are they doing now? On weekends most are locked into cells except for meals or mingle in an overcrowded yard."

"Mind if I jump in here?" Sawbucks said, red-faced. "Just want to remind you, there are armed guards, sharp-shooters, posted all along the walls overseeing the area where these games will be played, sir."

Corbett's eyes narrowed into a glassy stare while he looked at Sawbucks, as if his mind had traveled somewhere else. Then, with a slight cough, he sat up in the chair and said, "I'm a small dot on the landscape canvas here, Dan. Having just arrived to serve my first term, I'm really not well-acquainted with most of the senators. Other than the expression of distaste sent out over the air waves by our governor, we do have a problem assuring the citizens of this state that allowing the prisoners a sports program is not giving them more freedom."

"Of course and all I'm asking is a chance to at least allow them space to vent their frustrations on the playing field."

"I'll read all these letters and submit the proposal to my colleagues, but I can't give you a definite yes or no at the moment. Also, this will take some time."

"Well, that's all I'm asking for, sir, a chance."

As they parted, the senator smiled. "You know, I can really see your side of this."

Out on the street, Sawbucks looked dejected, "Didn't sound good, did it?"

"I don't agree," Dan said as they began looking for a taxi. "He's obviously not a friend of the governor who adamantly opposes this program. So, I think that he might consider backing it for that reason. That's politics."

"I can't see any politician running on a pro-convict's platform, Dan."

"Maybe you're right."

That night, unable to sleep, Dan walked through the Garden Beautiful to the Porch where he stood smoking, listening to the reassuring calls of the night watch that all was well. *The prison was crouched low, like a sleeping jungle cat with one eye open,* Dan thought, as he turned and walked back into the office.

After a sleepless night spent at his desk catching-up on work missed during the trip to the capitol, Dan waited in his office for Fetcher who arrived, sheepishly grinning and saying, "Morning, sir. Is this the right time, sir?"

The Kitchen area, a small cluster of buildings hunched down between the prison and the bay, included the doctor's office, hospital and another small building containing the holding cells where death row inmates were housed on the night before their scheduled execution.

Although not a religious man but one who also believed in covering all bases, Fetcher made a sign of the cross as they hurried along a brick path interlaced between the shrubs and flowers. Through the open door, they could see the doctor sitting at his desk and as Fetcher led the way, peering around the door, eyes wide with fear, Dan followed and closed the door.

Croaker acknowledged Dan with a slight nod and turned to Fetcher, saying, "Yes? What is it?"

"I was told you wanted to see me, sir." His hands were trembling clutching the cap.

"Yes, yes." The doctor waved a hand, impatiently. "I'm offering you a chance, for once in your wasted life, to better yourself."

Fetcher hung his white-fringed ebony head, studying the rumpled cap he was twisting in nervous hands and said, "Yessir, I been told about it and sure appreciate your kind offer but I wants to stay here 'cause this is my only home, sir, and the Loot, here, says so, too," glancing under his eyebrows in Dan's direction.

Croaker leaned back in the chair, hands crossed behind his head, scowling and said, "Let me make myself clear, Fetcher. The Loot has no say in this matter. Now, I understand and I'm in sympathy, but the law states emphatically that you must be released. The patient taxpayers of this wonderful state are sick of supporting you! I'm offering you a good home in town and your duties will be simple, as befitting your mind."

"Yessir," Fetcher said. "But I surely didn't know that the taxpayers were supporting me."

"Indeed they are!" Croaker snapped, irritation crimping his words. "Who the hell do you think supports this god-forsaken prison?"

Glancing over at Dan who remained by the door, Croaker sighed deeply. "Well, nevertheless, I shall not argue with you. This is your last chance. I don't think you have much choice, Fetcher. If you don't accept my offer, they'll send you out there into that cold world, anyway, with two dollars and a handshake!"

Fetcher shifted nervously from foot to foot, sending an anxious look over at Dan who, unable to help him, nodded and smiled a little encouragement.

"Guess there's no choice, sir."

"Does that mean yes?"

Fetcher nodded, a tear sliding down his cheek.

As silence invaded the room, Fetcher remained standing, head bowed, waiting for dismissal.

"You may go now. There will be certain conditions to this job which I'll explain later." Croaker was glaring at Dan who walked through the door with the dejected prisoner.

The next day, Dan frowned, asking one of the clerks if Fetcher had checked out yet.

"Yessir, he came through while you were at lunch, Loot."

"Was he with the doctor?"

"Yep, the poor guy."

"Strange, but I have a feeling we haven't seen the last of Fetcher." Dan said, smiling.

The sun had just burst across the bay, juicing the morning in an orange haze when Informer entered Dan's office carrying a copy of his latest edition of the Mews. The editorial read: "Here's an item for all to ponder. Someone recently noted that the gas passing through the tall flue from the new gas chamber, forms a crooked cross as it rises into the atmosphere. The warden, who refused to endorse this form of punishment, might make a note of this omen."

"Now what the hell are you stirring up?" Sawbucks asked, slamming his coffee cup on the desk.

"What the hell did I say that offends you?"

"You didn't need to make that remark about Rogers," Sawbucks said, huffing, dropping his feet from the desktop and tossing the paper into a waste basket.

"Ah shit, Sawbucks, this is giving him a chance to reply to all the rumors circulating about the fact that he never attends the dances anymore. Last week he went on a trip and we had to suffer Whistler again."

"When's your parole?"

"Hey, not soon enough. That's why I'm here. I'm due for a parole hearing soon and if they give me the nod, who's going to be me?"

"Nobody if we're lucky."

Dan, looking up from the paper, said, "There's someone I have in mind and I hate to say it but he'll never have your spit and fire. In spite of that, I think I'll recommend him anyway."

"Who is he?"

"All I can say is that he's almost as smart as you and, more importantly, he's doing a long stretch."

"If I have to train him, I should know his name, Loot."

"No. Because, I know that you won't like him anyway. So, I'm sparing myself all your bellyaching down the road."

"Lots of time, huh?" Informer wore a puzzled expression on his face as he lit a cigarette. Then, remembering something, he snapped his fingers, saying, "Speaking of time, were Croaker's boys ever punished?"

"Not yet. Rogers hasn't decided whether to give them solitary or the Hole. Which do you think they deserve?"

"Deserve?" Informer laughed. "They deserve a medal, Loot. They drank up all his booze and splashed in his pool until dawn when the cops arrived on complaints from the neighbors saying the acoustics were keeping everyone in the neighborhood awake. And they came back willingly to prison, happily soused and sated."

"Yeah," Sawbucks said, shaking his head. "Croaker denies the car keys were left on his desk. And did you hear that he billed the prison for the booze and food the boys consumed?"

"Yeah, but I heard his claim's been denied and he's under investigation for carelessness, as well."

"This investigation might uncover some other interesting facts, too." Informer hinted as he tossed the cigarette into an ashtray and started out the door when Dan said, "Incidentally, Rogers has decided on a week in solitary for all of them."

"What about Croaker?" Informer had a slight grin as he glanced over at Dan and Sawbucks, who ignored his remark.

"The one I wonder about is the guard at the gate who waved them off in the doc's car while they're still in prison stripes. He's been suspended during an investigation."

"Yeah, said he thought they were actors here for that movie scheduled next month."

"It was pretty clever of them."

"I don't know if it was clever of them or they just decided to go for a ride and couldn't believe the guard waved them on through. They had no weapons."

"So, with no place to go and no money, so what the hell and Croaker's house was just up the road."

Sawbucks was laughing so hard that some of the office staff stopped working to stare. Realizing this, he quickly shuffled some papers on the desk, glaring over at them.

When the Mews printed Informer's rendition of the escapade, Sawbucks saw no humor and angrily called him over to the office, asking, "What the hell did you print here?"

Informer shrugged, lit a cigarette and rebutted with his usual sarcasm, saying, "What's wrong with it?"

The editorial read: "A group of the boys from the hospital staff borrowed Croaker's car one balmy evening and drove into the sunset, waved along by a great big friendly salute from the guard at the back gate. Later found at Croaker's house, swimming, eating and drinking into such an intoxicated state that they illuminated the skyline and woke the neighbors. But, the boys protested, they were released through the gate by a guard who thought they were actors so they decided to play the part."

Informer also referred to Croaker as *Doctor Tokay* and his residence as *The Distillery*.

Croaker flew into a rage, asking Rogers to shut down the paper and send Informer to the Hole. Jake later related this to Dan who agreed to accompany Informer over to the warden's office, angrily shouting, "Goddammit, Informer, when will you learn? This might cost you a parole!"

For once, Informer was mute and after Rogers chastised him for ridiculing a prison official, he agreed to print an apology to Croaker in exchange for a suspended sentence of two days in solitary confinement.

"I apologize to the good doctor for referring to him in my last communication as Dr. Tokay. However, it was pleasing to learn that his requisition for full reimbursement of the cost of the liquor and food the boys had consumed was denied. The warden emphasized that such carelessness must be punished, apparently referring to the fact that the doctor somehow misplaced his car keys."

Once again, on the following day, the doctor flew into Dan's office in a rage, waving the newspaper. "Do you call this an

131

apology?" he yelled. "He's insinuating that I gave the cons those keys! Why doesn't he question the guard's actions at the back gate, huh?"

"The guard's been suspended during the investigation," Dan said as he glanced across at the office staff. "And, besides, he did apologize, didn't he?"

"Apologize? How can you say that? That con has never apologized for anything in his whole life, including the reason he's here. He probably blames that on someone else too, like maybe his victim."

"You know, you're right. He does blame his victim."

Croaker stood for a few minutes, momentarily stunned by Dan's remark and then said, "That's the first thing you've ever said that made sense!"

As he stormed from the office, the slammed door was his farewell.

Chapter XIII

The morning had begun under a sudden squall shaking light snowflakes like dandruff off the shoulders of the storm and graying the day as Dan walked across to the warden's office. Since snow flurries were a rarity, the prisoners were awe-struck upon emerging from their cellblocks and seeing the white-washed mountains staring back.

"Well, Dan," Rogers said, greeting him with a smile, "we just got the coroner's report on Canary and it's just as I thought, he died of natural causes. The heart ceased functioning and close examination showed severe deterioration of arteries. He can't answer your question about missing organs because the body had already been sent to the mortuary before we sent in our request. However, he says if there had been missing parts, he would have noticed so there probably wasn't anything unusual about the body. What the hell did he mean by diseased or missing body parts?"

"There are rumors about Croaker that have been circulating ever since I came here."

"Do you believe rumors from cons, for Chrissakes?"

"No but it's always safe to investigate."

"Well, I hope you're satisfied."

"No, I'm not. This report raises a lot of questions in my mind. It still leaves a possibility of murder here."

"Aw shit, Dan! I'm not borrowing trouble. I'm accepting this coroner's report as fact and putting the entire episode to rest."

"I'm wondering how well these two doctors know one another."

"What the hell is that insinuation?"

"Not insinuating, sir, just questioning."

"And I said it's finished!"

"Yes sir."

Whistler came through the door just as Dan turned to leave and said, "Is there a problem here, sir?"

"No," Rogers replied in an irritated way.

At the door, Dan turned and asked, "Say, what's happened with Fetcher? Is he still with Croaker?"

Rogers shrugged and said, "As far as I know, it seems to be working out for him in town."

"Good. He's been there longer than I thought."

"Really? You expected him to run off?"

"Yeah, something like that." Dan sighed as he closed the door, and, walking along the smooth floors, wondered again why Croaker wanted Fetcher, knowing his belligerent attitude toward the old man.

"Doc does have a wife, Dan," Sawbucks had said later as they sat in the officer's mess having lunch. "I heard she's been in a wheelchair for years."

"What happened?"

"Not sure. I think that she had a stroke or something."

"Is there anyone else in the house?" Dan asked with a worried look in his eyes.

Shrugging, Sawbucks took another bite of his sandwich. "Why? You don't think Fetcher would do anything stupid, do you?"

"With these guys, you never know."

"Maybe we should check on him, huh?"

Dan rose, tossing the napkin on the table, saying, "Think I'll drop in on Croaker," and walked away, leaving a puzzled Sawbucks staring after him.

"My wife?" Croaker said with a puzzled expression on his face. "Why do you want to know?"

"Just heard she was ill and wondered how she was."

"She's dead."

"Oh, I'm sorry." Dan stood by the office door for a few minutes.

"Anything else I can do for you?"

"Well, just wondered how Fetcher was working out."

"As well as any feeble-minded man can. I really believe that I made a mistake with him."

"Send him back, if you feel that way."

"Shit! They won't take him back here or I would!"

Dan smiled with relief as he walked back to the Porch. He just wasn't sure why, however.

The line of men was strung along the Porch and down the brick walk, patiently waiting for Dan and Sawbucks to process them on this rainy morning. Evidently the sky had lowered its shade as a storm advisory was heard crackling on the office radio. It had been several months since Dan had spoken to Croaker and he had totally forgotten Fetcher until a grinning face greeted him as he glanced up from the paper work.

"Howdy, Loot."

"Fetcher! What the hell are you doing back here?"

"I got sticky fingers, Loot."

As Dan scanned the file, he read aloud, "The doctor's gold watch and a gun? You stole them and held up a liquor store in town? What the hell were you thinking, Fetcher?"

Grinning, Fetcher shrugged, saying, "Just wanted to come home, sir. And the doc, he just ain't got no sense of humor 'cause I gave him the watch back and anyway, the gun was old and rusty. Why, that store clerk laughed at me 'fore he took it away and called the police."

"But Fetcher, you're not a thief."

"I am now, sir. They gave me twenty years."

"That should take care of the rest of your life."

"Yessir." He chuckled and said, "But the taxpayers ain't gonna like it."

"Well, we won't tell them this time." Dan smiled. "Okay, move along, your old cell is still vacant. You haven't been away

135

long enough to rent it out. And this time you'll be in charge of the back gate."

"Thank you kindly, Loot. Thank you kindly."

As he left the office, he did a sprightly two-step to the surprise of the men waiting in line.

A few days later, Dan met Croaker in the mess and asked, "Why do you think Fetcher went to work for you, Croaker, when he could have had a general parole somewhere else?"

"Why don't you tell me?"

"I think he knew that by working for you, he could easily be sent back here on any violation. By taking a general parole, he was chancing being sent to another town in the state and another prison on a violation."

"What's so funny?" Croaker was trying to understand Dan's broad smile.

"If you want to know, it's simple. When Fetcher knew his parole was coming up and realized that he would have to leave, he put on that act."

"What act?"

"Oh, maybe being a little more feeble-minded and forgetful than usual and not knowing why he was here, for instance."

"So?"

"Only someone like you with all your fancy psychology training would be so smug as to tag him feeble-minded and he knew that. Someone else would have seen him for what he really was, a very smart old man." Dan said, smiling.

Croaker's face grew livid. "Are you saying that cagey old con outsmarted me? Did you know that gun was a Civil War antique, very valuable, and now it's missing?"

"Sorry about that." Dad said, struggling to keep a straight face.

Dan could see the anger rising in the man and for a moment felt pity but brushed that away quickly, remembering Croaker's attitude toward the prisoner.

A few days later, Informer sauntered into the office, "Hi Loot."

Dan turned away from his paper work, saying, "Now what?"

"Think I know why Croaker wanted Fetcher working for him. I've got a story but I need more proof before I can print it."

"Well," Dan said, turning back to his work. "When you get it, let me know."

"Don't you want to hear it?"

"No. Not unless it's been authenticated."

"Well, that's going to be hard to do unless you can raise the dead!"

Dan laughed, saying, "I've been known to work a few miracles but not that one!"

Turning away, Informer glanced across at Sawbucks who was listening and said, "Hey, Sawbucks, would you be interested in this story?"

"Not unless it's been checked and re-checked."

"Okay, guess I'll have to sit on it for a while."

After Informer walked back along the Porch, Sawbucks looked over at Dan, "Wonder what that was about?"

"Don't know but maybe I'll check it out," Dan said and walked from the office along the path to the hospital, passing another long line of fish waiting to be processed.

Croaker was reading a journal, legs crossed and resting on the desk when Dan entered the office, closing the door softly.

"What is it?" Croaker didn't look away from his reading.

"Just have one question for you. Why did you pick Fetcher to work for you when you detested the old man?"

"That, sir, is none of your business."

"Well, Informer is sniffing out something here that involves this hospital and possibly you. If you have anything to hide, better spill it now."

Dropping his feet off the desk, Croaker glared at Dan, then lit a cigarette and blowing out the match slowly, eyes narrowing, said "There's nothing that Informer could say that would hurt me or this hospital, I can assure you."

Looking into his cold eyes, Dan said, "Good. I just wanted to be reassured about that."

On the way back to the Porch, Dan stopped at Informer's office. "Okay, Informer, what is it?"

"I thought you weren't interested."

"I wasn't. But after some thought, I decided that maybe you did have something. I know how Croaker felt about Fetcher and so I wondered why he would want the old man around his house when he detested him."

Informer laughed, saying, "That's exactly what I thought and then I did some snooping and found this!"

He held out an ink-smudged letter that had been wrinkled into a ball and said,

"This was found inside a waste basket in my office."

"Could be a hoax, you know."

"Maybe, sir, but I don't think so. Do you want me to read it to you?"

"I think I can manage that."

After reading the letter, Dan started to walk away, saying, "You can't print this, Informer."

"Why the shit not?"

"Because I said so, that's why."

Dan walked through the door, slamming it and creating a few moments of inquisitive stares from his staff.

In Rogers' office, the three men stood silently as the warden read the letter then tossed it on the desk. "Where the hell did you get this?"

"Informer said it was found in a waste basket in his office but has no idea who put it there."

"It's obviously been written by Canary. It's signed by him. Does this mean he knew he was going to die?"

"That's hard to say," Jake said. "After reading it over, all it says is that Croaker's not to touch his body. It could mean anything."

"But why would he ask the doctor not to touch his body after his death?"

Rogers was drumming his fingers on his desk. "Well, the only way we'll know what this means is to get Croaker up here."

Pushing a button on the desk, he summoned Whistler who rushed into the office, saying, "You wanted me, sir?"

"Yes. I want you to get Croaker and bring him here."

"Now?" Whistler shot puzzled looks at the others.

"Now, and make it fast."

Watching Whistler leave the office, Jake turned and walked to the windows. "I don't get the connection. If Canary knew he was going to die, he might have contemplated suicide."

"There was no evidence of a self-inflicted wound, Jake, according to the doc." Dan looked across the room at the men who seemed to be in shock. "And that brings into question Bags' suicide, doesn't it?"

Silence moved into the room, caught in the footlights of the drama unfolding, as each man contemplated the situation.

"Jeesus!" Rogers let out a deep breath. "What the press will do this with! Cons are committing suicide right under our noses!"

"Or murder, right under our noses!"

At this moment, Whistler and Croaker came through the door. "What the hell is this?" Croaker's face was red, a large vein throbbing in his forehead.

After reading the letter, he threw it down. "Well? What's this to do with me?"

"Why did he say you weren't to touch his dead body?"

Shrugging, he said, "How the hell do I know what cons mean? He was a nut, anyway."

"He worked in the hospital for you, didn't he?"

"That means nothing! A lot of cons have worked there off and on over the years. I don't remember him."

"Strange, but he remembered you."

"What do you mean by that?"

"Your name was the last word on his mind before he died."

Silence trekked around the room again, kneading the air, brushing against glass windows clouded with stale breath and tobacco smoke.

The jute mill's sharp whistle announcing the end of the work day screeched through the office like a corroded needle on a phonograph record as Rogers went to his desk to remove the wrinkled letter and place it inside a locked desk drawer. "We'll get back to this tomorrow, Croaker."

The bay was a chilly gray chalkboard this evening, as if contemplating a short nap between storms. Even the gulls were quietly swooping along the hushed shoreline in their eternal search for food, forgetting the usual noisy squabbling.

Dan and Angel were sharing a weekly dinner, sitting at a window watching the evening creep across the waters of the bay while a woman on the beach below hovered over two small children playing in the sand.

Ham Crane approached the table, pointing his cane at the scene on the beach. "Families of inmates, trash! Cons shouldn't be allowed any visits!"

"That would ease our workload a lot but the poor devil's need some reason to live."

"I see old Angel here has gotten some of his screwball con's advocate philosophy across to you. Take my advice, don't go soft on cons or you'll be asking for Walrus's fate," he said and limped away, cane tapping on the floor.

"I'm delighted to see that old Ham acknowledges my presence," Angel said and laughed as he reached for a salt shaker. "However, it's my opinion that Walrus's fate was due to his own hard line."

"I still wonder why Ham hangs around here," Dan said, looking across the room at the table where Ham was sharing a meal with another man. "There's nothing here for a man who's too old to be employed at the prison."

"Don't know. So, he's very eccentric, a loner. What were you thinking?"

"Just that it's a gloomy place for retirement."

"Agreed, and I have never found any record of his employment here, either. Odd."

"Maybe he was an inmate, not an employee."

"Jesus!" Angel laughed, and said, "If that's possible, all the more reason for not hanging around!"

"Well, he could be Topper." Dan was smiling as Angel stared at him, eyes narrowing, glinting in the last rays of a setting sun.

"You are a strange one, for Chrissakes! There's no Topper. Can't you get that through your head?"

Informer was standing in the warden's office on the following morning when Dan and Jake entered. Rogers was sitting at his desk, smoking a cigarette and reading a morning newspaper.

"This story's hotter than my uncle's pants in a cat house on Saturday night," Informer said, gesturing toward the desk where Rogers was holding a letter.

"Croaker's on his way and we'll hear his side of this, first."

At that moment, Croaker and Whistler walked into the office as Croaker said, "So, what's the problem here?" He was glaring at Informer who returned the look with a grin. "Did you print something about me? If so, I'll sue. I don't give a damn if you're a con or not. Hear me? I'll sue!"

"Not Informer this time, doc," Rogers said, "The city newspaper." He handed the morning paper to Croaker, who read: "The serious problem at the prison regarding our infamous inmates was brought to our attention recently when the body of a dead prisoner arrived at a local mortuary with missing organs. Where is the rest of the body? A reporter was sent to the scene where he saw, firsthand, the shell of a man."

Rogers was nervously drumming his fingers on the desktop, smoke pouring from his nostrils as he tossed the cigarette into the ashtray and said, "How long has this been going on?"

"I have done nothing illegal, I assure you, warden," Croaker said, lighting a pipe with shaking fingers.

"You sound like Dracula, for Chrissakes!"

"Listen, I have studied under the greatest minds in Europe and I'm seriously researching the fountain of youth, that's all. Those men were already dead when I removed their organs. These are experiments that are going on right now, today, in Germany, sir. The greatest scientists in Europe are working toward a general well-being for aging men that will restore their sexual capacities. While they are researching for the rich, I am doing the same for the poor, that's all."

Nervously puffing on a pipe, he added, "How the hell did I know this con had a family? I only used the bodies going to Boot Hill, I assure you!"

In the silence, Dan said, "Well, this explains why you've been working here for such little pay. You're turning a prison into a laboratory."

"You could say that. I hoped to accomplish a miracle. I've been removing bits of testicles from the young corpses and implanting pieces of these glands into older men who, incidentally, are volunteers. When I can't get human material, I could use animals such as goats but I prefer humans."

"That explains why you wanted Fetcher, right?" Informer was now looking smug.

"He wouldn't cooperate, the old fool!"

"I want to know what body parts were missing." Rogers' anger was now replaced by fear.

"The heart, brain and testicles are gone, according to this newspaper." Jake said, reading from the newspaper article.

"The paper's wrong," Croaker said. "I only used the testicles."

"What the hell were you thinking" Rogers fumed, "putting this prison on the front page of every newspaper in the country?"

"I needed volunteers and in order to get cadavers to supply the organs, I relied on the cons who died in prison as well as the ones who were executed."

"How many operations have you performed?"

Shrugging, he said, "Never kept track but since I came here, I would say," clearing his throat, "uh, several, maybe ten or twelve. I worked at night, on my own time, so I didn't charge the state for any of this work."

"Do you have any idea what problems you have caused? You've been messing with imprisoned men who have no rights!"

In the silent office, voices from the hallway were heard and an occasional whistle or distant foghorn infringed upon the thoughts of the men.

"Have you been successful?" Jake finally asked the question on everyone's mind.

"Yes. The old men have seemed happy with the results."

"I want a list of their names." Rogers was still unable to comprehend the situation, adding, "Do you know that you've been messing with men who would have no way in hell of testing your goddamned results, anyway?"

"Ah, sir, you have it wrong. This was not just for their libido. No, it's for their general health, mainly."

"Jeesus! I'm going to be crucified in the press!" Rogers' face had evolved from slightly red into livid purple. "I want their names, those old ones."

"Yes, I'll provide that. Some, of course, have passed on, but very happily, I assure you."

"I don't want your goddamned assurances, you ass!"

Croaker rose from the chair and calmly knocking the pipe sharply against an ashtray, asked, "Do you want my resignation now?"

"I don't have that authority." Rogers said and swiveled around in his chair. "It'll be up to the board and I'm sure the medical association will be investigating."

Croaker nodded and then walked from the room.

Informer turned, with a smug look. "Well, you guys wouldn't listen to me. Now, I've been cheated by that city paper."

"That's too bad. I wouldn't let you publish it anyway," Rogers said and was furiously tossing papers around on his desk when the phone rang. "I guess that will be a summons for my resignation!"

Dan and Jake walked slowly back to the Porch, each lost in thought when Jake said, "You know, I always agreed with the cons when they refused to go to the hospital even when sick as dogs."

"Sure. They knew all along but wouldn't divulge it. Wonder why?"

"That's their code, Dan, the prison code."

To everyone's surprise, Croaker was only temporarily suspended while his case was studied by a medical board. He was later reinstated when it was discovered the organs from the dead man had been donated to a hospital for implanting into a charity patient. The item in the city newspaper read: "The dead man who had been a cold-blooded murderer was found to have done one decent act at the end of his life which has redeemed him in the eyes of the public as well as his doctor."

Informer had the last say in his editorial: "The question is, did the dead man agree to this maiming before he died or did the doctor wait until the prisoner could either agree or disagree? Having known Canary during his few years here, I say that he was vehemently opposed to having his body mutilated, even in death, and he left this message in a wadded, crumpled-up note found in my office."

Because of the publicity, Croaker submitted his resignation a few weeks later, claiming that he needed more time for his research.

"What do you think?" Sawbucks asked as they were in the office discussing the scandal.

"About Croaker? He could have been involved in more than just mutilating bodies for his research. There are many unanswered questions here. For one, his diagnosis of Bags' death as suicide is questionable because it seems like a rush to judgment. On the other hand, it could be just his way of dispatching any problem quickly. Get it out of the way and move on. Who knows?"

Dan remained on the Porch for a long time with many unanswered questions racing through his mind.

Chapter XIV

San Francisco

The Chinatown Brigade, an elite group formed over seventy-five years ago in the city, consisted of several city policemen, hand-selected by the chief of police, himself. Unfortunately, some police had become jaded over the years, dipping into cash registers on occasion and intimidating shop owners. These were men Angel was familiar with in his line of work and were not necessarily liked by him either but after all, *money is green* as he always said when asked to represent them in court.

In recent years, however, a new police chief in San Francisco, in an effort to establish better relationships between the Chinese and the local citizens, established a committee of merchants who were friendly with their counterparts in Chinatown. Thus began a feeling of camaraderie shared by the Chinese merchants with regard to the city of San Francisco who now began hiring Chinese men to be trained as police officers, eventually patrolling the streets of Chinatown which pleased the shop owners.

On this overcast morning, Angel was lugging his heavy briefcase across Grant Avenue on a trek that began on the corner of his street in a vain attempt at flagging down a taxi or jitney. Late for a court date, he was rushing along, cursing, occasionally glancing over a shoulder in hopeful anticipation, thinking, *where the hell were all the cabs, for Chrissakes*? At this sweltering moment, a squad car pulled alongside the curb and Angel spotted a smiling young Chinese officer leaning over and opening the door on the passenger side, saying, "Hey, Angel! Need a ride? Slide in!"

As Angel happily slid into the seat, he murmured a grateful, "Thanks." Then, settling into the cushions, he looked at the officer, saying, "To what do I owe this? It must be my bubbly personality!" When the man didn't answer, Angel looked into his face and said, "Hey, don't I know you? Of course, you're Chan's son-in-law, right?"

The young man at the wheel merely nodded and drove slowly along Grant Avenue until he made a sharp wide turn into an alley, skidding to a stop before a jewelry store.

"Hey, what the hell.......!" Angel was being yanked from the car by unseen hands as he struggled to keep a tight grip on the briefcase, out of habit. In this early morning light, there were a few people on the street and those passersby never looked in his direction as Angel was hustled through the door into a dark shop that tinkled with wind chimes. The last thing he remembered was a breeze blowing wind-chime soapy bubbles and thinking, *is this my Wash Day?*

San Quentin Prison

Peter Stone was rock-salt hard, a brittle man, sharp-voiced, tough and as wiry as a ropedancer. Having lived for years in the hardscrabble part of the Arizona desert, he resembled in some ways a twisted saguaro that had been struck by lightning and "as mean and nasty as any critter found out there," in one guard's opinion.

During his tenure as sheriff in a small town in Nevada where rattlesnakes outnumbered citizens, Rogers had met Stone briefly and was impressed by the man's ability to handle tough prisoners. Stone's duty as a deputy sheriff in a town so desolate that it had to import its water supply through a wooden flume from another town, had ended with the supposed murder of a ranch hand who had been briefly jailed on charges of attempting to poison the flume water and later found suffocated in his cell. Since this cowboy belonged to a local Indian tribe, the uproar was heard across the state when Stone was exonerated of the charges in a trial that brought the Indians out in tribal dress, carrying torches and burning Stone in an effigy that contained a rock heart.

This angry confrontation forced Stone to seek employment elsewhere, declaring, "Those damned Indians still think they own the state. Time they learned that they don't mess with Pete Stone."

However, despite all his tough talk, it was not the Indians who left the state.

"I brought in Pete Stone as a temporary guard but hopefully on a permanent basis," Rogers said at the staff meeting on this Monday morning. "And he will be here serving as my assistant with Whistler during my absences."

Dan could see this was a surprise as well to Whistler who seemed very subdued at the meeting, leaving abruptly without joining in the welcoming greetings.

When Stone first strolled through the prison yard in a ten-gallon hat, chewing on a piece of hay and looking for trouble, the inmates quickly tagged him.

"Tombstone is an appropriate name," Informer said, smiling, "for a man looking for a home on Boot Hill." And he quickly added, "Which I think he'll find soon."

"I don't like his weapons," Dan said, watching the man strolling across the Garden Beautiful.

"He's not carrying a weapon, Loot."

"Yes he is--his fists."

It wasn't long before stories, reeking like foul breath, began drifting through the prison about Tombstone's use of the Hole.

"Where's Nick?" Dan was looking through his files when he suddenly looked over at the office staff.

"Nick?"

"Yeah, that little Flip who occasionally cleans my place whenever the idea strikes him."

Several of the men glanced away while others began opening file drawers and began busily typing.

"Well?"

At this moment, Sawbucks came into the office and seeing the unusually busy staff, looked at Dan, saying, "What's wrong?"

"Well, it seems no one knows what happened to Nick."

"Nick?"

"My house cleaner who didn't show up this morning to clean my place."

"Sorry Dan. He's in the Hole."

"What the hell for?"

Sawbucks shrugged. "Don't know. With Tomb, er, Stone, who knows?"

Tossing down the papers, Dan walked from the office and the staff suddenly became quiet.

"Hey, you guys get back to work unless you want to join Nick." Sawbucks said, wondering, *why would Stone put that innocuous little runt in the Hole?*

The Hole had been a form of punishment in the early years of the prison and although it still was in place near the edge of the bay, it was seldom used. On occasion in those days, guards were known to have tossed in sacks of lime, resulting in destroyed lungs and tuberculosis that became rampant during those early years.

In the warden's office, Dan met with Jake and Whistler, saying, "I heard Nick was in the Hole and I want to know why."

Jake shook his head, saying, "No one's used the Hole, Dan, in years."

"Well, it's being used now."

When there was no response from either man, Dan turned and walked from the office toward the area behind the hospital where the Hole was situated. Grabbing a prisoner who was weeding, Dan said, "Here, help me open this lid."

"Yessir," he said and the prisoner straddled the iron cover of the Hole as Dan grabbed the handle and they were able to wrench off the rusted cover which rolled across the graveled path. Peering deep inside, Dan saw Nick crouching low, eyes blinking. "Okay, Nick, come on out of there!"

As Nick hoisted himself up, Dan was furious, saying, "What the hell did you do?"

"Nothing, Loot, I swear." Raising one hand in the air and coughing, he began trembling. "It's cold down there."

"Well, it had to be something. I need to know, because I'm confronting the man who dropped you in there."

"Yessir." Nick was looking around, almond eyes blinking. "Well, he told me to clean the latrines, sir, and I said I only dust."

Dan had trouble keeping a straight face as he asked, "Where were the latrines?"

"Those in the mess hall and I guess all of them, sir."

"What did you do to make him give that order?"

Nick shrugged, saying, "Nothing, Loot, nothing." Pausing momentarily, he mumbled, "Maybe told him to clean them himself, maybe?"

"Okay, come with me." As he turned away, Dan motioned to the prisoner standing by the Hole and said, "Put the lid back on."

"Yessir."

In his office, Dan issued Nick a pass, allowing him to leave the yard for the small bungalow situated across from the school grounds. As he watched Nick walk away, Dan remembered their first meeting several years ago when Nick, wrapped in an enormous white apron, stood at the door of the bungalow, announcing, "I come to cook for you, Loot."

"No," Dan had said. "I eat at the mess. You clean and then return to the main kitchen."

But the little prisoner stubbornly remained at the door, eyes not flinching, saying, "I'm only good at dusting."

"Okay, you dust, then return to the prison mess hall."

But Nick remained motionless, staring at Dan.

"Are you deaf?"

"No sir. I heard you but I only dust. Don't like kitchen work." He was shaking his head vigorously.

"You mean you don't like that four letter word."

"What's that?"

"Work! Okay, stop playing dumb and deaf and get to work. Then at noon, report to the officer's mess."

Grumbling under his breath, Nick had walked into the small house, slamming the door as Dan began walking toward the prison remembering that Nick was a harmless prisoner who was serving time for burglary, and, with his friends, waiting to be returned to the Philippines at the end of their sentences.

On the morning following Nick's release from the Hole, Tombstone walked through the Porch, pushing aside the line of fish, and entered Dan's office.

"Is this how I'm to be treated here? My orders ignored? A bastard con lipping me! Huh?" His face was livid but his voice was low and harsh like a croupy frog.

Dan looked up from his pen, inking-in a fish's status for the jute mill, saying, "If you're referring to Nick, the prisoner you placed in the Hole, I won't tolerate that punishment on my watch and everyone knows that."

"This is insubordination," Tombstone was sputtering, face twisting in anger.

"If that's what you want to call it, sir."

Abruptly turning away, Tombstone walked back through the door and slammed it.

The office staff collectively held their breath as Dan continued working on the papers for the waiting fish.

Back on the carpet again became a routine song by Dan's office staff, with one inmate threatening to make it the theme song for the prison. Sawbucks was pacing the office floor after Dan walked over to the warden's office when he noticed Informer lounging along the Porch railing.

"Now, what?"

"Hey, Sawbucks, you're beginning to sound like the Loot."Informer teased as he lit a cigarette and with a pen began writing in a small tablet he was carrying.

"What are you saying now?"

Before he could answer, Dan walked back along the Porch, entered the office, followed by Informer, and went to his desk. Looking over at Informer, he started to say something but was drowned out by Informer's parroting "What do you want" and adding, "nothing, Loot."

"Okay. You answered your own question. You have my permission to leave."

"Not before I find out what happened this morning."

"I'll never tell you."

"Oh, shit! Guess I'll have to worm it out of Whistler."

Somewhere in the office, one of the staff began whistling a tune and the typewriters began humming again.

Leaning back in his chair, Dan looked over at the office staff, saying, "Nothing happened."

"Thanks. Guess I'll leave."

Sawbucks who was filled with curiosity and unable to restrain himself, said, "Come on, Dan. What happened?"

"Nothing happened."

They soon learned that Rogers was away in town for a week-long session with the dentist. When Dan had walked into the office, Whistler informed him that the matter of the Hole was still under consideration until Rogers' return.

Dan also learned that a letter had been sent informing the board of Tombstone's behavior in ordering men dropped into the Hole for several days. The anonymous letter was sent to Cardoza, who decided that although the board had never taken an unsigned letter seriously, there were enough complaints about this man to immediately suspend him. The board's letter to Stone stated that, "If you care to challenge this, sir, we will be happy to hold further hearings on this matter. In the interim, we will withhold your earnings until such time as a future date is agreed upon. Or, if you prefer to accept the wages, the matter will be closed."

Apparently, Tombstone decided to accept the decision not to debate his dismissal and checked out at the front office, leaving no forwarding address.

Rogers returned from a miserable week, having endured the loss of most of his teeth and, with a swollen face, lisped, "Where the hell is Stone? I buzzed his office but got no reply."

Whistler, Dan and Jake were in the office for their weekly staff meeting on this Monday morning. Whistler, unable to completely hide his smug look, spoke first, saying, "Sir, the gentleman was discharged by the board on Friday."

"Why the hell wasn't I informed of this?"

"We were unable to reach you and besides, you, like all of us, have to accept the decisions of the board, sir."

Standing by his desk, Rogers looked stunned. "I know that for Chrissakes. What I want to know is why he was fired."

It was now Jake's turn to say, "He'd been exceeding orders on punishment, sir, by sending men into the Hole without a final check with you or Whistler."

"Oh." Rogers sank like a deflated balloon into his chair and said, "I thought the Hole was abolished years ago."

"Apparently it was not, sir."

"Well, it does serve a purpose for the hard ones, you know." Rogers looked thoughtfully across the room. "And I'll certainly miss my old friend, Stone."

Dan, over the next few days, wondered about the anonymous letter that had been sent to a member of the Board and also Tombstone's abrupt departure.

"Somehow, I see Whistler's fine hand in this." Sawbucks said, chewing on tobacco as he looked over at Dan. The office was quiet during the lunch break with the staff at the mess hall. "Who else would know a board member's name and address, Dan?"

"Maybe it was Topper?"

The foghorns were bellowing warnings for any craft braving the choppy waters this evening as Dan walked from his office. Waiting to be checked out through the inner gates, he decided staying late at the office created problems with the night shift who were barely acquainted with one another.

The ten o'clock notes of the bugler's *Taps* echoed mournfully across the prison walls, seemingly to rise from the bogs of some forgotten battlefield, as one by one, the lights of the prison were gradually extinguished.

The long night watch had begun as uniformed men stood along the walls, silhouetted against the darkening sky like shadowy musketeers from another battlefield, shouting in hollow voices, "All's well," as each man paced his territory and watched the play of lights along the prison yards below.

The sharp screech of a riot whistle brought Dan back to the gates just as he was starting toward his home.

"It's in the west wing!" A guard was shouting as he raced past Dan who quickly spun around and followed.

At the cellblock, Roller Skates, rifle grasped tightly in both hands, shouted, "They're raising hell in there."

Dan led the way into the cellblock. It was total chaos. Mattress stuffing was torn and strewn around the cells and along the tiers, burning stubs of cigarettes were smoldering along the walkway while men shouted obscenities, raised fists banging tin plates against the iron bars. One of the guards was pelted with feces thrown from a tier above and as he cursed, raising his rifle in that direction, Dan grabbed the rifle. "Go back to the showers. We'll handle this without guns."

The stunned guard turned away amid shouts from the cells, "Hey, you fucking screws! You give us shit, we'll give you shit!"

"Okay," Dan yelled at the other guards. "They're covering-up something." Seeing the line of armed guards calmly approaching in orderly fashion, the prisoners began to settle down with mumbled curses.

"Hey Loot," a voice beckoned from above. "Better check on a guy up here. Think he's almost dead."

Dan started up the steps, motioning to Skates who had a key to the cell door. The man was sprawled across a lower bunk, writhing and moaning as Dan bent over him.

"Get a stretcher and get him to the hospital!"

Turning the prisoner over, Dan looked into a bloody face and said, "He's alive."

"What's wrong?" Skates looked down at the bundle of blood.

"He's had his tongue cut off."

Skates gasped and leaned against the bars. A figure in the shadows of the cell watched intently as Dan grabbed a towel and covered the man's face, pressing down hard on his mouth.

"Look for the tongue."

The hapless guard began searching the floor of the cell with a flashlight, signaling with a shake of his head, "Nothing here."

153

Glancing over at the cringing prisoner in the corner leaning against the toilet, Dan, deciding the search would be fruitless, said, "Okay, Sammy, let's have it!"

"What?" He was shaking so hard, his knees were wobbling when he stood.

"I want the knife and a name."

"Saw nothing, Loot, I swear! I was sleeping."

After the stretcher carried the moaning man from the cell, Dan ordered Sammy Sing, still shaking and whining, taken away for questioning. The cell was thoroughly searched by the guards, including removing a loose brick but nothing incriminating was found. Dan walked over to the window and looked down into the bay where the knife had obviously been thrown.

"He'll live," the doctor said.

The new doctor, a rotund man with balding head, was only serving temporarily until the position was permanently filled and was already ruing the day he volunteered. Tossing down the black bag, he dropped into a chair in Jake's office on the following morning, sighing deeply before lighting a cigarette and said, "Goddamn, why is it always on weekends? I missed my golf game. Shit, these damned cons do this deliberately. They don't want us to have one minute of relaxation."

"Hell, doc," Jake said, smiling. "You say rest? What's a golf game when these cons can provide us with barrels of fun?"

"You know, this guy won't ever speak again. Why? What did he know?" The doctor, looking across the room at Dan seated in the corner of the office, said, "Why not kill him?

"Maybe mayhem serves as a more gruesome warning to any stoolies than outright murder."

"It had to be the cellmate," Jake said.

"Sure, Dan's involved. But there had to be two men to hold him down. He's a big guy." The doctor squirmed in his chair, flicking ashes into a brass ash tray. "It could have been over sex, probably was."

Across the prison yard, a heavy lid was raised and the little man was shoved into a damp black hole. As he squatted, he looked up into the faces of the guards and smiled.

"He won't talk," an orderly wisecracked as Dan entered the hospital room where Auditor was strapped into the narrow cot.

"Why is he tied down?"

"We had a time with him when he came to, sir."

Dan looked at the man in the bed, placing a hand on his shoulder, "Hell, Auditor."

Agonized eyes searched Dan's face then closed as tears seeped down his cheeks.

"If I get a pen and paper, will you tell me about this?"

Auditor shook his head vehemently as his eyes swept across to the other bed where a prisoner was sleeping.

"He's out cold. Just came from surgery."

The bandaged face turned away, ignoring Dan who remained for a few more minutes, then walked away.

"Goddamnit!" Jake exploded when they met in his office the following morning. "You know he won't talk because he still has five more years. So, do as I suggest that we plant something on that bastard in the Hole. What difference does it make whether it's fabricated? We know he's guilty of mayhem, or anyway, of aiding in it. Work the way they do, Dan. An eye for an eye and in this case, a tongue for a tongue!"

Dan listened quietly to the shouting but decided to play the waiting game that he had learned so well from his astute instructors, the convicts, who knew the value of patience.

"I can see that you'll do it your way and not follow my advice. So, good luck."

The note found beside the dead man read: "I have no reason to live."

"How did he die?" Dan was standing by the bed in the infirmary when the doctor walked into the room.

"How the hell would I know?" Turning away, he yelled, "Get a slab in here."

The frightened orderlies rushed in with a stretcher and lifted the still warm corpse.

"That does it!" Jake pounded his fist on the table as ashtrays and pencils jumped in unison. "I will not believe that a helpless man strapped into a bed was able to get pills from a locked

155

cabinet in the infirmary and swallow them with his mouth on fire!"

The doctor sputtered, saying, "Damn, Jake, I've been trying to quit smoking. If I have to listen to you much longer, I'll take it up again. Now, you don't want that, do you?"

"I don't give a tinker's damn if you quit eating whale blubber! I want to know how that dead man was able to get a bottle of contraband pills!"

"For one thing, he wasn't dead at the time and I already told you, I don't have any idea how he got those pills!"

Dan, quietly listening as the doctor and Jake continued bickering, said, "Maybe an orderly felt pity, Jake. Stranger things have happened in this place."

Jake sneered, saying, "D you think a con would feel pity for another con? Dan, you got to stop having dinners with that radical, Angel!"

"Aw, come on, Jake," Dan smiled. "Angels aren't radicals, just peace keepers. Besides, now that you mention it, I haven't seen him in a while."

Chapter XV

The usually noisy yard was subdued, even downright glum, on the morning Dan led Sammy from the dungeon where he had been placed after two days in the Hole. With eyes blinking like a startled owl, he stumbled walking between Dan and another guard as they crossed the yard to Jake's office. Dan wondered if Auditor had been a scapegoat for some escape plan gone awry or had stumbled upon something, maybe the identity of Topper? Somehow, today, dejection and gloom hung in the air like a sweat-soaked blanket and Dan wondered what was bothering the men.

"Hey," Sammy was trembling as Jake stared at him from behind his desk. "I ain't done nothing, I swear! I was asleep when I heard the cell door open, that's all. Didn't see or hear nothing. It was pitch black in there. Before I could get down off the bunk, it was over for the poor slob."

"Come on you little pissant," Jake shouted. "No one has a key to the cells except a guard."

Sammy shrugged and said, "Then I guess it was a bull!"

Jake leaped across the desk, grabbed him by the collar and as his fist swung, the sound of cracking bones echoed in the room as blood spurted from the Sammy's nose and mouth.

"Nobody accuses my men, especially a piece of shit like you!"

Sammy was wiping his face with a tattered sleeve as he blubbered, "I'm saying again that I didn't do it or see it."

As Jake raised his fist again, Dan stepped in. "Okay, that's enough."

Jake paused, stared at Dan and, turning away, wiped his fore-head. "Get some towels in here, he's ruining my rug."

"I'll get him to the infirmary and then we'll be back." Dan had Sammy by the arm and was leading him from the room when the prisoner staggered, falling against the door. Just at that moment, the door opened and a guard came through, leading an orderly from the hospital.

"Want me to take him, sir?"

"Yeah," Dan said. "Get him into the infirmary and after that, back to the dungeon."

"Aw shit, Loot!" Sammy whined.

The guard hesitated and then Jake yelled, "Get him outta here!"

After they left, the orderly stood by Jake's desk, asking, "You sent for me, sir?"

Impatiently wiping his hands with a handkerchief, Jake looked at the prisoner. "You know goddamned well I sent for you! Stop playing your little con games with me and spit it out. Who got to Auditor?"

Glancing across at the doctor who was lighting a cigarette, and then over at Dan, the orderly twisting his fingers, said, "I don't know how he got the pills. I went on my dinner break and when I returned, he was, well, uh, unconscious."

"Who relieved you?"

Perspiration formed in tiny beads on the man's forehead as he said, "No one, sir."

"What?" Jake bellowed. "I thought we had definite rules that the ward be manned at all times."

"Yessir. But we only had a few patients and this guy was strapped in. We decided that two men weren't needed until the ward swelled."

"Yes." The doctor shifted in his chair. "That's true and that's the way it was when I took over. They asked to be relived for short periods of time and I said it was okay since the former doctor had set those rules. I'm only a temporary employee so I saw no need to change any rules. We do have a shortage of medically-trained help, you know."

"You're right. We have a shortage of trained men of any kind, period!" Jake was still seething. "Okay, doc, just because an empty bottle was found beside the bed doesn't mean that's what killed him. So, we need that autopsy, sorry."

The doctor nodded as he rose from the chair and walked to the door, cigarette still dangling from his mouth.

"Hey doc," Jake shouted. "You forgot to put out that cigarette."

Pausing at the door, he snatched the cigarette from his mouth, tossed it in an ashtray with a lopsided grin. "How the hell did that get there?"

Three days later, Jake called Dan over to his office.

"Well, the autopsy shows the pills didn't kill him. Doc found a needle mark on his arm and on further investigation,, it seems that Auditor had been given a fatal injection of morphine. That means someone with medical knowledge. Who else could use a needle?"

"Oh hell," Dan offered. "Lots of cons are users and ex-users, you know."

"Maybe some are former or even present users?"

"Or, the most likely one would be an orderly who could get around the ward unnoticed or a friend of an orderly."

"I think we should check on the orderlies in there as well as any friends."

"Incidentally, the family claimed the body today and as far as I know, they are unaware of his mutilation. Just were told that it was an overdose."

"All hell will break loose when they get the report from the mortuary." Jake heaved a deep sigh as he sat back in the chair.

As the days passed, there were no reports of any investigations by the prisoner's family.

"Evidently, the mortuary accepted the doctor's story of an accidental overdose and never bothered to examine the body." Jake looking relieved, sighed. "However, this leaves an unanswered question to the puzzle of who did this, and why?"

Sammy served one week in the dungeon and although still adamant about Auditor dying by a guard's hand, was sent to work on the farm. A few weeks later, Sammy was killed in a freakish tractor accident, witnessed by several inmates who claimed they saw him deliberately fall under the moving tractor.

"With such reliable and trustworthy witnesses," Jake said. "How can we question this unfortunate death?"

Although Auditor's puzzling death joined that of Canary and Bags in Dan's mind, Sammy's death seemed to positively prove that he knew who killed Auditor. The morning dawned with the first wave of fog creeping away, shaking filmy robes as an eerie silence rolled through the cellblocks where thousands of men waited for the tolling bell to set them free.

"Who's the bird in the gas house today?" Informer was casually leaning against the office door, pen in hand. Before anyone could reply, he snapped his fingers, "Oh shit! I forgot why I'm here. Stone's back!"

Dan and Sawbucks looked over in surprise with questioning eyes, saying, "He's back here in the prison?"

"Well, one foot in the door, maybe."

"You don't say!" Sawbucks whistled.

Shrugging, Informer, with a smirk as big as the bay out there, rattled on, "It's just a rumor but I heard that Rogers has tended his resignation and recommended Stone as his replacement."

"Are you the cat or the canary?"

"Loot, what does that mean?"

"Well, you seem to have been in at the meetings between those men and from your smug looks, I just wondered if they had consulted you."

"Hey, don't blame me, for Chrissakes! Just because you know there's no hope now with Tombstone in there, for that playground of yours, right?"

Dan simply stared at Informer who looked contrite. "Sorry, Loot, I didn't mean that." He walked back through the door, hesitating on the Porch for a few minutes before disappearing.

"Wonder what'll happen with the Hole." Dan and Sawbucks were having coffee after Informer had retreated to his own office.

"Nothing, now. It looks like we'll be going back to the good old days." Dan seemed disconsolate as he lit a cigarette, blowing the smoke slowly. Then, rising from the chair, he looked through the windows toward the garden. "And it looks like I'll be playing the waiting game again."

Informer's reference to the gas house brought back memories as Dan walked along the Cakewalk this morning. When the state legislature had passed a bill to replace the gallows with a gas chamber, a guinea pig was needed for the test. In his editorial that week, a spoofing Informer had asked for volunteers and, surprisingly, received several. All were on death row, of course, and all agreed to be a guinea pig on a written agreement that in event of a test failure, they would be pardoned. Since the state refused to play the game, an animal was selected from the farm. Unfortunately, they had selected the wrong animal. Porky, a piglet born on the farm, had become a special pet of the prisoners and there was a loud protest when he was placed inside the chamber with a plate of peaches. The test failed and the piglet emerged, unscathed, waddling across the floor and collapsing in a guard's arms. Severe stomach cramps were diagnosed by the doctor and double jeopardy was diagnosed by the prisoners.

"Porky has been reprieved to serve out his life sentence on the farm while gaining immortality by being the only one executed to live and oink about it," Informer wrote. "As for the rest of us, the newly installed gas chamber is in full working condition."

A week later, Rogers received an unsigned letter, saying, "Thanks warden for saving the first dance for me. Too bad it wasn't a tango for two, me and you! Signed, Porky."

Rogers was furious, waving the letter at Dan and Jake as they entered his office. Tossing it down on the desk, he said, "It was mailed in San Francisco. How would anyone over there know about the piglet?"

They never learned the identity of the letter writer although there were numerous suggestions.

Today, in the brightly-lit cell, overhead bulbs cast an eerie glow as Dan entered, accompanied by his shadow hunching along the dusty walls like a specter from a Charlie Chan movie. In the tobacco-scented air, a rotund man, reclining on a bare mattress was contentedly smoking a pipe, curls of smoke skimming along the ceiling, as he contemplated a chess board set on a stool. On the wall an autographed picture of the *It Girl* was pasted. Owlish eyes blinked through wire-framed glasses and a smile of recognition passed across his lips. "Howdy, Loot, glad you could make it to my last curtain call."

Rising from the cot, the former actor knocked ashes from his pipe onto the floor. "Thanks for my glasses. I couldn't get through this last game without them. I've been playing a guy in the city through the mail."

"Anything else you need?" Dan asked, seeing no point in conversation, an experience gleaned over the years.

"No sir. At the moment I'm looking at God's feet but soon I'll be looking into His eyes!"

"Maybe you need a chaplain?"

"I am my own chaplain and my own executioner."

The door opened and the new doctor, Robert Byrd, tagged Birdcage, stepped inside the cell, with his bag.

"Give him a shot of whiskey." Dan pointed to the black bag the doctor had set down on a stool.

"I prefer scotch."

"Only have whiskey, sorry," Byrd said as he opened the bag and poured the whiskey into a glass.

Dan turned and walked down the corridor toward the gas chamber where a large man was slouched against the wall like an apparition of Atlas. Extending his hand, Dan smiled. "Glad you could make it, Rogers. I thought you were gone!"

"The board hasn't settled my resignation yet, dammit! And, of course, the governor rang this morning. He may delay this execution."

"That's strange. This man wants to go."

"It's the family, I hear."

"His family?" Dan was incredulous, saying, "He murdered his mistress and the family is upset over his execution?"

"People do surprise you, don't they? Curiously, he's had no contact with them since he's been in here."

The sharp peal of the telephone on the wall echoed along the quiet halls like a school bell summoning students.

After a brief conversation, Rogers hung up the phone and said,. "Okay, Dan, proceed with the execution."

The line of witnesses walked along the corridor like a covey of quail, heads bobbing in chatter, eagerly straining to shut out the grim surroundings.

Dan heard the familiar harmonica, saw the procession led by a barefoot prisoner escorted by two guards and smelled the stench of death. Garbed in white shirt and pants, the prisoner waited patiently while a stethoscope was taped to his chest and a long tube attached to it. Having refused a blindfold, he glanced around curiously at the spectators, pausing briefly on the face of his victim's husband.

When the pellets hit the ground, smoke poured forth, he turned toward Dan, began to speak and his body suddenly lurched back in the chair. For several terrible moments, Dan watched this strange man, who had welcomed death so eagerly by defying all attempts to save himself, struggle desperately against the restraints, eyes bulging in fear, mouth screaming muted words that seemed to be *help me, help me*! On the following day, the newspapers blared in large type: "The movie actor, who for months had begged to die, changed his mind at the last second. In the act of dying, he discovered life."

The waters of the bay were tracing fingers across the sand, ebbing and flowing in an eternal pattern as Dan walked along the shore that evening in the shadows of the prison. He was reflecting on the years that had passed since his arrival and remembering there was still no ball field tucked away under those shadows. A trip to the city over the weekend brought little hope of help from his friend, Paddy.

"I just can't tell you anything definite. You know the times are hard now with money really tight."

"I don't need money, Paddy. Just some support from those people in the legislature."

Paddy sighed. "I know, and I'm doing what I can for you."

"Not enough, Paddy, not enough." Dan felt defeated.

"What's that mean?" His voice had a suspicious ring to it.

"Paddy, stop living in the past. You sound like you think I'm threatening to expose you."

"I thought no such thing, Dan, never." Paddy rose from the chair and reached for a bottle of whiskey perched on a shelf over the sink. "So, let's drink to friendship. Speaking of which, how is your friend, the prisoners' advocate?"

"Oh, Herb Angel. You know, I haven't heard from him or even seen him around the prison in a long time." Dan frowned as he sipped the whiskey. "Guess I should look him up but have no idea where to start."

"That's easy. Start at the prison. Isn't that where all his friends live?"

"Good idea." Dan laughed. "Yep, that's where they all live. He never met anybody on the outside he called a friend."

That evening on the ferry back to the prison, Dan decided to locate the attorney but had no idea where to start. Angel had never mentioned a home and if he had an office, it was also never a topic of conversation.

"Bluebeard wants to see you, Loot. Has a confession," the dry voice crackled and snapped over the wires as Dan sleepily answered the phone but the line went dead before he could speak. Checking the clock he saw the time was three in the morning and he had been awake until midnight, unable to sleep. No prisoner was up at this time, even the kitchen help slept until five, so this had to be someone outside the walls. The voice had a familiar ring, a clipped accent, which Dan tried to place as he dressed and walked toward the prison etched in bright, silver-plated moonlight.

A shadow bounced off the wall, fluttering through the dense brush that lined the path leading to the Cakewalk. A sound as faint as a bird on the wing caused him to turn slightly just as a blow to the head crumpled him to the sidewalk. A few hours later, waking in the hospital with an aching head and the faint memory of a raised arm holding a hammer, Dan asked the doctor what had happened.

"You had a close call." Birdcage was sitting on the bed in the hospital as he leaned over with a flashlight looking into Dan's eyes, saying, "That blow could have crushed your head, Loot."

"I remember hearing something and turned my head in that direction so the hammer must have just grazed me."

Sawbucks was standing in the doorway. "I've come to take you home, you lucky son of a gun."

Holding his bandaged head and limping toward the car, Dan wasn't thinking lucky, he was thinking angry. "Why the hell would someone want to kill me?"

"Hey Dan, we're all targets. But, you of all people! I don't understand that, either."

Recuperating at home, Dan puzzled over the incident and especially the voice that had summoned him to his *Wash Day!*

When Dan returned to work, Sawbucks greeted him with, "We can't find the weapon. It's probably in the bay by now."

"I just wonder if my attacker was a prisoner."

"Huh?" Sawbucks looked shocked. "What? You don't mean a guard!"

"Who has access to the yard at that time of night?"

"Aw, for Chrissakes, Dan! Not one of us! Besides, if they wanted you dead, you'd be there now. It looks to me like it was a warning or something."

"You're right. It could have just been a warning."

"And it could be someone jealous that your athletic program may be making headway."

"A lot of people there," Dan snorted. He couldn't put the thought away. *Stone blamed him for his earlier dismissal and Whistler had been an outright enemy from the first day. Whoever lured him out that night was as guilty as the perpetrator of his attack.* Dan was now more surprised than angry at the thought that he had such an enemy in the prison. After all, he knew those who were opposed to his sports program and they just weren't capable of doing something this potentially fatal, or so he hoped.

Bluebeard Jones was reclining on his cot by the Cakewalk studying a horoscope and sucking on a lollipop when Dan entered the cell. Placing the book down, the prisoner sat up and said, "To what do I owe this honor?"

Standing by the door, Dan leaned back against it, saying, "Last week I received a phone call saying that you had a confession to make before you die. I assume you were plagued with guilt and confessing to your crime, right? Anyway, on my way over to your cell, I was attacked in the yard. Know anything about that?"

"How would I know anything, Loot? I'm locked in here day and night. So, do you wanna search me for a phone?"

Dan lit a Chesterfield, passing the white cellophane package over to the man who grabbed several with stubby fingers, hungrily stuffing some into a pocket and one into his mouth. As they both watched the smoke curl around in spirals with no place to go, gradually settling around the cell, he reluctantly said, "Thanks for the smokes."

The mole-eyed man, built like a wide window low to the ground, was clad in the ill-fitting uniform of the condemned, loose clothing with no belts, buckles or buttons.

While the two men studied one another, Dan picked up the horoscope that Bluebeard had been studying. "Believe in this stuff?"

Bluebeard replied in a testy tone, "Don't believe in much, Loot."

"Why do you think I was lured over here last week?"

"How would I know?"

"You only have a few months to live. Why don't you cooperate and maybe I can help you."

"How can you help?"

"Well, you once wanted a reporter to interview you," Dan said, blowing a circle of smoke while studying the man. "So, I'll see what I can do about that."

Bluebeard perked up and said, "I wanna tell my story. I guess everyone wants to hear how I killed them. I never told it in court or anywhere. It'll make a great movie."

"Then, you were sent up on circumstantial evidence?"

"Yeah."

"In exchange, you'll also give me Topper's name and if he ordered that attack on me."

Bluebeard moved uncomfortably on the bed. "If you get me a reporter, you want me to name this here Topper fella?"

"Yes."

"Okay," he said as he shifted on the bed. "It's a deal. I'll name him when you escort that reporter into my cell."

"Okay," Dan said and turned to leave. "But I'm curious. If the story's about how you lured rich old women into your home and killed them, who'd want to see it?"

"Hey, lots of people like to watch other people getting erased!"

"Is that why you killed, just to watch a woman die?"

Moving restlessly on the bed, Bluebeard smirked, saying, "Hey, I ain't talking till I see that reporter."

The phone had an insistent ring this morning as Dan entered the office. Jake was calling from the Cakewalk. "Bluebeard was found dead in his cell this morning."

Slamming down the instrument, Dan raced over to the Cakewalk where a few guards and inmates had congregated. Inside the cell, Birdcage was bending over an inert form as Whistler stood nearby, wringing his hands. "We'll catch hell for this! The state won't want to hear that he's dead, for God's sake! What about the scheduled execution?"

"Oh crap!" Jake shouted. "We'll just have another one."

One of the guards snickered as Whistler glared over at him."

"What happened?" Dan was staring at the inert form.

"It looks like he choked to death." Birdcage rose from the bed. "We'll need an autopsy for this one."

Later, in the hospital, Dan, along with Jake, watched the autopsy and to everyone's surprise, Birdcage pulled out a long string of soft pliable sucker sticks which were crammed deep into the throat.

"Looks like the lips were sewn together with twine after the sticks were shoved into the throat. Obviously done while unconscious," Birdcage said and frowned, wiping his hands on a towel.

"I want to know how they got into that cell," Jake angrily shouted, "and where was the watch?"

A nervous guard stepped into the room from the hall and said, "I was on duty last night, sir."

"Were you on all night? Did you take a break at any time?"

"I was on from midnight to now without a break, sir."

"Do you have your thermos with you?"

"No. I sent it back to the mess about an hour ago."

Birdcage was drawing a sheet over the body and looking over at Dan and Jake, frowned, saying, "I'm only guessing but I think the guard's coffee might have been drugged and he slept through the murder."

"Murdering a prisoner, even one on death row, will bring an automatic death penalty to the perpetrators," a shocked Jake said with clenched teeth.

Then, the trembling guard exclaimed, "Aw shit, Cap'n, they only killed off a bunch of bad chromosomes, in my estimation."

"Shit!" Jake was shaking now in anger as he looked at the guard. "Don't let this get out or we're all in trouble but I agree with you!"

In the silent room, a ticking clock continuing on its journey, also testified to life.

"Death by asphyxiation," the official autopsy report read. There was also a small amount of a narcotic found in the man's bloodstream but not enough to cause death.

"Considering his size, it would have taken more than one man to drug him," Rogers said as he studied the report. "Somebody had to sit on him!"

Dan said, "He was obviously drugged as well which means the coffee was spiked by someone on the kitchen staff that night.

So, I think Bluebeard was probably doped by the coffee also and the cup taken from the cell."

"That makes sense," Rogers said as he lit a cigarette, exhaling deeply, "due to his size. So someone could enter and leave that area without being discovered since the other cells were empty and the guard was knocked out."

Leaving the administration building, Dan walked with Jake over to the Porch. "Looks like Bluebeard won't achieve the immortality he wanted, after all."

"How do you mean?"

"He wanted a film made of his life, thinking that would make him immortal, I guess. I just can't understand a man who tortured elderly women thinking that would make a great movie."

"He brought out their maternal instincts, you know, with those lollipops he was always sucking. That's how he was caught, I understand, a lollipop found under the body."

"Well, he'll be immortal around here for a long time due to the weird way he died. He choked on lollipop sticks."

"Yeah, makes a good movie title," Jake said as they parted. "How about suckered to death?"

Chapter XVI

San Francisco

The sound of splashing water mingled with fishy odors swimming in a musty vinegar sauce, its fumes clogging his nostrils, greeted Angel as he awoke. Looking around, he saw only murky blackness and heard only the slap, slap, slapping of water under the floor. *What happened and where the hell am I?* From the sounds and smells, he decided it must be an abandoned warehouse along the waterfront. Reaching for the spilled briefcase whose contents were strewn across the floor, Angel then felt his aching head, which, to his immense relief, seemed to be fine. Yanking at the vest pocket looking for his watch, he attempted to read the time but that was impossible.

Deciding it was probably smart to grab the briefcase and get the hell out of here, he began walking, pressing against the walls. Just then, a door opened, throwing a long narrow shaft of light into the empty warehouse. A large man in a silk robe was outlined peering into the room, looking like a blister full of pus, Angel thought, as he pressed tightly against the wall. At about that moment, Chan spotted him, saying, "Mister Angel. How are you feeling, sir?"

His voice had that polite oily overlay, that purring smoothness so unctuously flattering and so perfectly trained that Angel long ago knew this was not an act. This was part of the man's character, diligently honed over the years when dealing with the people in this part of a world so distant from China.

"Mister Chan, sir, I am fine. Thank you." His voice was hoarse and cracked, with dry lips and sore throat aching for a glass of cool water. Both men remained still, silently watching, neither one making a move and barely breathing.

Casually lighting a cigarette, Chan blew smoke in Angel's direction, causing him to cough, and with a shake of his arm, tossed away the match saying, "I did not intend to harm you in any way, sir." His voice was low and silky. "But I knew that would be the only way to see you. You are a very stubborn and a very foolish man, sir."

"In what way am I, Mister Chan?"

Chuckling, he said, "In the way you repay debts, sir."

"You erased them, sir."

"Indeed I did." He was shaking his head and smiling now. "And I expected to be repaid for my efforts. But you continued to ignore my pleas, sir."

"What?" Angel's voice registered surprise and anger. "I never heard from you, sir. Indeed, I waited and then decided you forgot and I wasn't going to remind you. That would be foolish, don't you think?"

Chan threw back his head, laughing, saying, "You are, I know, a great attorney in court and there, you do stretch the truth, I've been told. But not with me, sir. Not in Chinatown. You are lying when you say I never contacted you."

It was Angel's turn to laugh now as he said, "Mister Chan. You are a true gentleman but you are the master truth stretcher. I never heard a single word from you. If I had, do you think I would have been trudging down Grant Avenue this morning?" He paused, cocking his head in a questioning way, "It was this morning?"

When Chan nodded, Angel continued, "Carrying my brief case? Would I have stepped into that squad car driven by your son-in-law?"

Chan remained on the threshold, quietly in thought then said, "Are we saying the same thing? Someone has bamboozled us, is that it?"

Angel laughed, saying, "Well, it seems that way. Now, shall we discuss this strange situation and how to remedy it?"

Chan moved through the door, walking toward Angel as he spoke. "And what do you propose, counselor?"

San Quentin Village

Ham Crane nodded as Dan breezed through the swinging doors of the café, propelled by gusts of wind. Autumn with its tantalizing fragrances of crackling eucalyptus and pine in the wood stove, embraced the room, two-stepping with the pleasing scent of chicken fricassee on the stove taunting everyone's palates.

Angel rushed through the door, stopping to warm his hands, rubbing them together over the stove before joining Dan at the table.

When Angel had rushed into his office last week, Dan was not only pleased to see him but surprised and demanded, "Where the hell have you been? I was about ready to send out a posse."

"Hey, you sound angry." Angel was smiling as he pulled up a chair, placing the briefcase on the floor and using it as a foot rest. "Ah, hell, I needed a trip away from all this," he said as he waved an arm in a wide arc. "And I found a great fishing hole over there on the coast. I will take you sometime, Loot, if you ever decide to untie the apron strings here."

Dan laughed, saying, "That will happen once I accomplish my goal. And a fishing spot sounds like just the place to celebrate."

"It's a bear out there on the bay. Going to be a long cold winter and it's only October!" Angel sighed as he sipped the beer then said, "Dan, have you ever heard of a bed-wetter psychiatrist?"

"That's a new one on me. What is he, a children's doctor?"

"I heard it for the first time today, myself. I have a client who called his court-appointed psychiatrist, a bed-wetter, and some other words which I've never heard before, either. So, I asked him what the hell it meant. Found out, to him anyway, these are people who practice in the north end of town over there on Nob

Hill, you know, never seeing the society along the wrong side of the tracks, so to speak. He says bedwetting, nail biting and hair-pulling are all traits of the more affluent in our society. So, he claims, what the hell do their doc's know about him and his rotten, lowdown life here in Q?"

Angel's bellicose laugh filled the room as some diners turned to stare.

Settling into his meal with a ravenous appetite, Angel paused between bites, saying, "How's your new place?"

Dan had recently moved off the prison compound into a small apartment outside the gates on a bluff overlooking the bay. It was so near Witt's End that the dinner menu aromas each evening invaded his apartment. "Never need to ask for a menu," he had told Louie.

"Hell, I needed some privacy and you never get that living inside the gates."

"That's true and it also makes it harder for them to find you in the middle of the night, right?"

Dan laughed and said, "A little, but they still do."

"Heard any more about Bluebeard's murder?" Angel looked casually across the room at Ham Crane's table as he spoke.

"Nothing since I came back from vacation. Why?"

Shrugging as he buttered a roll and, with a twinkle in his eye, glanced across the table. "No reason. Just have an idea."

Dan raised his eyebrows, saying, "You do?"

"Hey, don't look surprised. I earned my way through school as a private eye. Didn't you know?"

"No, but it doesn't surprise me. So, what about Bluebeard? What's your thought?"

"I already knew from some of my clients that Bluebeard's been a marked man since he hit the Bastille here. So, when they put him over there, he was being kept on ice until his execution."

"I didn't know that. But I wouldn't, anyway, since that's not on my watch."

"Yeah. Well, he was riddled for other reasons but not because of your reporter, Loot. Sorry to disappoint you."

173

Dan laughed and said, "Not disappointed, just curious."

Leaning over and speaking in a low voice, Angel took Dan by surprise. "I think he knew who killed Walrus."

"And he was going to blackmail someone?"

"Well, that I don't know. But he had lots of ammunition on someone in here and it's not a con."

"Do you think a guard?"

"How do you think he got the narcotics in his system?"

"Jesus! Not one of us!"

"Think about it. A con couldn't get a drug to him."

"What about his meals? He could get contraband that way."

"Sure. But that's unlikely because the kitchen staff is changing almost every day. No, Dan. It's got to be a guard or someone who works here and has access to the cells and the Cakewalk." While Angel continued with his meal, Dan snubbed a cigarette in the ashtray as Louie began clearing off the dishes.

"Not that," Angel exclaimed as Louie grabbed a plate. "Not finished because this is good to the last scrap, Louie"

"Why doesn't that flatter me?"

"'Because you didn't cook today! Saw the wife over there." Angel gestured toward the kitchen where a large woman stood in the doorway, angrily yelling, "Louie! I said no more for him!"

Angel, joining in the crowd's laughter as Louie escorted an inebriated customer to the door, muttered, "Thought for sure she meant me," and continued dunking a thick slice of bread into the gravy swimming on his plate.

Upon returning to his apartment, Dan reflected on his conversation with Angel, remembering Auditor's cellmate, Sammy Sing, who had insisted a guard was involved in Auditor's death, and then subsequently, walked into death. Dan went over the names of every guard he could remember who might have had recent access to Bluebeard and only three names came home to roost: Roller Skates, Tombstone and Jake. Skates had drawn night duty at the Cakewalk prior to the murder and Tombstone was covering the area as part of his newly-appointed watch which was also Jake's watch.

"Want him to cover every watch before I retire," Rogers had stated at the last staff meeting where Stone was received with as much warmth as a new fish being finger-printed. "And I want everyone to know this man is a good law enforcement officer as well as a close friend of mine. I'm glad the board had second thoughts and reinstated him."

As he spoke, there were several glances exchanged and eyebrows raised but no one spoke, either in greeting or condemning as Tombstone sat impassively smoking a cigar and nodding in agreement with the words of praise.

The prison was quietly poised, defiantly ignoring the erratic whims of the weather, wearing its dust jacket opened at the throat, revealing dark iron bars hidden deep within its belly. Then, without warning, the wind was suddenly aroused, sweeping across the bay, massaging the rocky shoreline, blowing sailboats around the choppy waters, belching debris through the air and churning wildly under the pilings of a pier by Witt's End.

In response to the sudden squall, the prison buttoned-up its dust jacket, closed the gates, summoned the prisoners in from the farm and hunkered down in imitation of the sodden-winged gulls who sought shelter within the coves and inlets.

"Hey, Loot." Informer was wearing the prison blues and a worn, gray cap acquired years before. "I feel as naked as a peanut out of its shell."

"That's interesting. What brought that on?"

"I've been paroled!"

Dan dropped the papers on his desk and Sawbucks stared open-mouthed, saying, "I'll be! I never thought I'd see that day!"

"Neither did I," said the jubilant prisoner who tossed his cap into the air. "Hey, this cap was issued to me when I entered this university of noxious misery. It's always been a symbol of defeat! And it will remain by my side for the rest of my life as a symbol of what can happen if you're not looking!"

"That's good. Where're you going?"

"I've been contacted by the publisher of a small paper on the coast. He's a great guy, an attorney as well, just in case," he said, smiling smugly. "And he's also arranged for my transportation and lodging."

"That's good." Dan said, smiling as he glanced through the papers of incoming fish on this blustery morning.

"So, Loot. Who is he?"

"Who is who?"

"You know who I mean."

"Oh, yeah, the new editor. He's almost ready."

"Will I meet him?"

"Sure. He's expected any minute. I sent for him when I heard the news of your parole."

As Dan spoke, a prisoner, frosted mustache coating his upper lip and appearing to have just stepped from a glossy magazine cover featuring a judge minus the black robe, walked through the door. Resembling a model on the cover of Men's Weekly, he imbued the assurance of a man with a strong sense of self.

"Aw shit! Not him! He's the damned shyster from Millionaire's Row!"

At this outburst, Dan laughed, looking over at Sawbucks. "I told you, didn't I? If I'd selected James Cagney, Informer would've said he wouldn't be acceptable either as an accomplished actor or as a prison newspaper editor."

Informer laughed as he glared at his replacement, Mouthpiece Malone, who returned the look with a knowing smile, saying, "Informer, I have no intention of filling your shoes or, for that matter, your swelled head!"

Mouthpiece was a native of the city, born in the avenues and honed in the ranks of the local church schools, eventually becoming a very impressive attorney known for explosive eloquent speeches during his trials. As a local boy who made it to the top rung of the ladder of life, the success went to his head and he grew greedy. As a result, he was accused of having a wealthy benefactor murdered and was sentenced to prison for the rest of his life. However, Mouthpiece didn't let this deter him in his pursuit for fame and fortune while he continued appealing his sentence behind bars until there was no money left. Eventually, he turned away from the pursuit of justice for himself and offered legal help to his fellow cell mates. However, in the future, it would be his eloquence that would make his tenure as the newspaper editor so inspiring. Often a beautiful phrase or sonnet would appear in the newspaper which he insisted was sent in by an anonymous poet. Once it was rumored that he helped the child of an employee in an endeavor to win an exciting newspaper prize. However, he refused to acknowledge this which seemed contrary to his oft-reported huge ego.

Informer seemed surprised at the man's icy attitude because he was usually treated with a certain amount of awe and respect, by both inmate and guard. This respect had originated in fear of exposure of *something* since most of the inmates and a lot of the guards had *something* in their life that might come out to haunt or taunt them. It was known that Informer was a man who refused to be intimidated, cleverly using the prison system to his advantage. Vague threats and innuendo's became a vital part of his vocabulary. He often quoted Angel's favorite adage by ending his news items with words of encouragement, "the prison is the bottom rung on the ladder of life. There's no place else to go but up! Remember that!"

Walking away, Informer shouted over his shoulder, "You fill my shoes? That will be in your dreams!"

Somewhere in the quiet office, an inmate began whistling and the others began typing in unison to the tune until Sawbucks glared at them.

"Wonder what all that meant?" Sawbucks looked across at Dan, who laughingly said, "Aren't you the one who's famous for the line, *who knows what anything means in here?"*

While the prison settled down to patiently endure an expected storm, a prisoner disappeared. Whistles shrieked and uniforms began racing through the grounds in a desperate search for Tubby. Several months ago, Tubby had heard there was going to be a conscription drive by the State National Guard and he appeared in Dan's office early one morning, saying, "I wanna join-up, Loot."

"Now why would you do that when you have such a good home here?"Sawbucks yelled.

Ignoring him, Tubby continued with his plea, "I was told that if I join up I'll get a pardon from the governor."

"Where the hell did you hear that?" Dan asked.

"I, I, uh, don't know, sir."

"The only word on that was in the Great War of '18, if you served in the Armed Forces and were killed in battle, it's possible that the governor would consider a pardon, if you had been a member of the militia at the time, Tubby. In other words, you'd not only have to be a hero, you'd have to be a dead hero!"

"Aw shucks, Loot, there's always a catch."

As Dan watched a dejected Tubby leave, he remembered the man was here because he had assisted in a murder-for-hire plot with his brother. Living in poverty in the San Joaquin Valley, his family had subsisted on following the seasonal crops, picking grapes, peaches and figs. He and a brother had been offered thousands of dollars for killing a rancher's wife by dumping a sack full of hissing rattlesnakes into the swimming pool where the woman was relaxing on an inner tube. Her husband, who had hired them, was also killed by the snakes as he hastily scrambled out of the pool, all the time shouting and cursing, "Goddamned fucking assholes! Wait till I get out.........................!"

The sheriff, in relating the incident to Dan, had a difficult time keeping a straight face, saying, "Talk about justice with a capital J, don't that say it all! And the worst of it is, Loot, that dumb kid keeps yelling there's snakes in his cell, all the time. Glad to get rid of him."

"And the worst of it is," Dan repeated, "he's still screaming in the cell at night about the rattlesnakes."

While the moon washed its face in the still waters of the bay several days after the storm had abated, Tubby's body floated into shore, riding the crest of the waves until it caught the attention of a fisherman who rowed out to examine the strange package.

When Dan arrived at the pier, Birdcage was bent over the body. "Damned thing is, he evidently attempted to walk across the bay with a homemade snorkel," shaking his head as he turned over the body. "See, the tube is wrapped around his neck and one hand's still clutching a deflated float made of a football bladder. Where the hell did he get that?"

"I know," Dan said sadly. "A box of donated equipment arrived last week for my sports program and I guess he got into it somehow."

"I'm always amazed at the lost genius here in prison."

"You think he was a genius?"

"He designed a primitive method that enabled him to walk under water, if only for a short time. That took some genius, don't you think? Causes you to wonder what he could have accomplished under a different set of circumstances in his life."

"And a different time," Dan added.

"You know, he could have made it to a nearby cove with better equipment because he had a good idea." Birdcage was staring across the water watching sailboats bobbing like corks discarded from a wild party on the bay.

How he was able to escape over a guarded seawall would be another mystery Dan stowed away along with many other questions. Dan walked back to the prison in thought as the doctor, toting his bag, remarked on the fleeting years. "It seems like I've been here just a few days. I'm about to give them notice, Loot."

Surprised, Dan stopped. "Why? You just arrived. You need far more experience with caged men, doc."

"You're right," he laughed. "But I'm going into private practice, taking chances I know, yet anything is better than this duty. It's too depressing."

Dan thought about this, wondering how one man could find this work so depressing and another find it so rewarding. "Just another rung on life's ladder, I guess," he said as the doctor shot a surprised look in his direction.

San Francisco

Paddy was standing on the corner of Grant and Bush, deep in Chinatown, watching a butcher in a bloody apron haggling with an old Chinese woman over the price of dried fish bellies. While they were yelling, she was pointing to the scales perched on a crate of oranges where the bellies were being weighed as he waved the apron around, fanning off clustering flies. Oblivious to the flies, she persisted in high-pitched bursts of Cantonese that could be annoying to anyone other than the butcher who continued smiling, nodding and flapping his apron.

The noon whistle at the Ferry Building screeched through the misty air, sending scores of children emerging through doorways into the street. *Yes,* Paddy thought, *instead of streets paved in gold, these streets in Chinatown are paved in people. Not just ordinary people but strange people with odd customs in dress and speech* and, for a second, he experienced that familiar pang of homesickness. The building he was leaning against housed not only the butcher shop but also an herb shop where bottles of preserved snakes and dried sea horses attested to his feelings about strange customs.

Glancing across at the clock on the bank building, Paddy realized it was time for lunch and walked toward his favorite restaurant, The Sea Horse. There, he would indulge in his favorite dish, Chop Suey. "Never heard of it in China," a friend on the police force had once commented. "Invented right here in Chinatown by one of our citizens."

Just as he turned into the doorway of the restaurant with the delicious aromas invading his nostrils, a hand grabbed his shoulder and a voice said, "Peadar! Peadar! Is it really you?"

Without turning, Paddy recognized the voice and his heart skipped a few beats. Indeed, it was someone from his rebel days. Faking surprise, he turned around. "Well, if it isn't Jeremy! Jeremy Gibson, isn't it? As I live and breathe!"

As the two men stood in the darkened doorway, sizing-up one another, the black lacquered door opened and a cool rush of incense-scented air enveloped them.

"Well, I was just about to eat. Join me?"

"Sorry, I can't but I would like to see you again and renew our friendship," he said as he drew out a pen and paper from his pocket.

"Right," Paddy said lamely, writing his address on the paper and handing it back. Watching the man disappear into the noon crowd, Paddy wondered what he was doing here and above all, what he wanted. They had never been friends, only acquaintances in a dingy Dublin jail on opposing sides of the war.

Chapter XVII

The prison was sunk in hushed silence along the bay on this moonless night as if in hiding, allowing only the splashing waves or screech of a gull to break the stillness. Suddenly, a crackling sound like a rifle shot reverberated across the prison walls, and the night became an inferno. Shooting red flames licked the licorice sky like bright tongues savoring the sweet taste and eager for more. The lone engine, manned by convicts from the prison firehouse, stood by helplessly watching the flames dance, two-stepping around the gray walls and whirling like so many ballerinas in class. Guards and prisoners raced around frantically with hoses and buckets to douse the fire destroying the jute mill.

"Like spitting on a volcano," Mouthpiece later wrote in the paper. "And the lava kept flowing while the beat went on until there was nothing left standing."

Along with the others, Dan watched in frustration as the mill burned to the ground. The fire posed no danger to the cellblocks but the smoke and stench lingered for weeks.

This jute mill which had kept the prisoners occupied for decades weaving raw jute into burlap sacks had shown a profit over the years with almost no competition from private industry. However, the constant racket took a toll on inmates and guards, while dust and lint contributed to damaged lungs. "Not a safe atmosphere for the men," Birdcage had lamented at an earlier staff meeting and had received only shocked responses from both Rogers and Tombstone. "What the hell! Are we worried about these killers getting sick, or something?" Tombstone said icily. "Hasn't this been a great means of supporting them? The state should thank us."

"It's true," Rogers was nodding in agreement. "So far it's kept the prison pretty self-sufficient."

Turning to Birdcage, he asked, "What do you propose we should do about their damned lungs, doc?"

The doctor seemingly slightly mystified, said, "What do I propose? I don't propose anything. I just said it was an unsafe environment which also includes your guards, Rogers. Maybe you should reduce the hours they spend in there, or something." His voice trailed off as he became more aware of the hostile atmosphere in the room.

"Or maybe," Tombstone interjected, "we could turn it into a spa and perhaps a great basketball court for the Loot here."

Dan was laughing as he spread his hands on the table, saying, "Now that's the best idea yet."

No one laughed with him and soon the meeting adjourned with Birdcage joining Dan on the walk from the room. "What do you think, Dan?"

Later Dan would regret his response but thought, *how can we mere mortals, foresee the future?*

"Well, I agree with you but you're butting heads against a "Stone" wall, just as I've been all these years with my ideas. I have learned something, though, from our jailed men and that's patience. It also keeps the blood pressure down."

Birdcage had already left the prison and gone into private practice in the southern part of the state before the inferno but Dan decided that wherever he is, he's smiling.

"It was deliberately set!" Whistler steamed and fumed as firemen had desperately fought it along with fire engines from town arriving after being summoned by the warden.

"We don't know that," Jake yelled in frustration and anger.

When a body count was taken, one prisoner was missing. Sparky, *Sparkplug*, a convicted arsonist, was not in his cell. Weeks later, while sifting through the rubble, human bones were found in the area where the mill door had stood.

"It's obvious that Sparky died in the fire. Is there any family?" Dan asked as he read the news accounts of the inferno.

"None that we can find. His file reads no next of kin."

"Herbert Angel was his attorney," Sawbucks said, as Dan winced.

While alleviating many health problems, the fire created other problems for the guards, with idle prisoners milling around the yards, bored and restless.

While this was occurring, the board appointed Whistler as interim warden until a man could be permanently selected to replace Rogers whose resignation was finally accepted.

"I'll never criticize any future warden," Rogers had said at his final board meeting. "This job doesn't pay enough to cover the hellish thoughts that creep into and corrode a man's soul."

With the mill gone and a critical need to occupy the idle men, road gangs were quickly formed and sent out to clear brush and litter from the highways while others were being trained in fighting forest fires. However, these programs only made a small dent in the number of inmates.

"There are plans to replace the old jute mill with a cotton mill. This will employ as many men, if not more and will be much cleaner," Whistler announced at the staff meeting following Rogers' departure. "Too bad Birdcage isn't here to approve," he added sarcastically.

An unexpected bonus for Dan playing through all this was the extra space the new mill would not require.

"Enough for an athletic field," Dan said, grinning, while Sawbucks snorted, "Fat chance, Dan."

"Well, it's worth a try. I'm sending a letter over to the board again. I think maybe this time, it'll work."

The morning edged toward midday and as the fog slowly retreated, whistles shrieked and prisoners clearing the rubble from the fire were each given a lunch in a paper sack.

Dan looked up from his paper work and saw Angel entering the office, briefcase in hand.

"Just wanted to know what happened with Sparky," he said, sounding breathless. As he pulled up a chair while chewing on a cigar, he casually glanced around the office. Since Dan knew there was nothing casual about anything Angel did, he assumed the attorney, from habit, was checking to be sure there were no witnesses to their conversation. Sawbucks, being the only one remaining in the office, leaned back in his chair reading the paper and gave no sign of recognition.

"All we have are a few bones resting at the coroner's in town. Why?"

"I think he should have a proper burial, don't you? Maybe just a marker on Boot Hill to show he passed this way once."

"I don't see any problem with that. I'll take it up with Whistler who's running the place now."

Angel let out a deep sigh, saying, "I know. It just isn't right that Sparky's totally forgotten even if he did burn down the mill. Not even sure of that. If it's true, he did both the cons and guards a favor, don't you think?"

"I'll see what I can do." Dan said, seeming distracted and Angel gave another long sigh, picked up the briefcase and left the office. Meanwhile, Sawbucks dropped the paper and stared after his retreating figure.

At the staff meeting that afternoon when Dan mentioned Angel's request, the room was quiet for a while, then Whistler, eyes wide with anger, hissed. "What are you asking? That damned con burned down the mill, for Chrissakes!"

"We'll have to put this before the board but I can't see any objection to sticking his bones in Boot Hill." Speaking with a slight tartness in his voice, Tombstone avoided Whistler's glare while everyone sensed the mutual animosity between the two men.

Whistler continued staring at Tombstone while considering his next words. "We'll have to let the board decide this, Mister Stone." Then turning to Dan, he asked, "Where are the bones, anyway?"

"At the coroner's in town."

After the staff meeting adjourned, Dan joined Jake walking across the street toward the front office. "What do you think about using the extra space after the cotton mill is completed, for a recreation field, Jake?"

"Thought you'd never ask," he smiled. "Why didn't you broach the subject at the meeting now?"

"I've already sent a letter to the board who will have the last word anyway. Until I hear from them, there's no point in listening to Tombstone and Whistler bellyaching about it. Also I think this mutual animosity between them will work for me."

Jake threw back his head and laughed so loudly that a few of the inmates working in the garden looked around.

Mouthpiece published his thoughts on the fire and Sparky in the Walled City Journal: "Where's Sparky? No one has seen him since the night of the inferno and I am speculating that he really didn't die in the fire but escaped over the wall while we were distracted in fighting the blaze. Maybe those bones are not his but belong perhaps to another unfortunate animal. If so, Sparky has achieved fame in being the only prisoner who ever successfully escaped this hell, one way or another."

Beyond the prison, high in the surrounding hills, a prickly breeze stirred the grass surrounding Boot Hill. A perpetual veil of fog shrouded the place where the cemetery rested. Weathered wooden crosses, crudely carved with names, dates or initials scratched in with a sharp knife, marched in rows across the hill. A thin wire fence hemmed the edge of the cemetery interlaced with stiff, whispering eucalyptus trees, like tin soldiers, keeping an eternal watch on the inhabitants. Some residents living nearby said they often heard moaning in the night, "A certain way the wind whistled through the trees," they would say while others claimed it was the tormented voices of the prisoners calling from their graves.

Dan and Angel joined the work party as they carried a small white box to Boot Hill.

"Well," Angel joked as he watched the box drop into a deep hole and quickly disappear into a blanket of damp earth and said, "Sparky's with his friends now, Loot."

"Maybe," Dan reflected, "if he ever had any."

They stood on the hill until the prisoners had tamped-down the earth and placed a wood cross with Sparky's initials carved into it, over the spot. Surprising both Dan and Angel, the two men stood with bowed heads for a few minutes.

"Okay, Loot," one laughed, saying, "if you don't need us no more, we'll just take off." He was pointing to the crest of the hill.

On their way back to the prison, Dan noticed that Angel was unusually quiet until they reached the Porch when he finally spoke, saying, "You know, time was running out for everybody."

The phone rang just as Dan was going to ask the meaning of that remark.

"Dan," Jake was on the phone, saying, "Need you to come over here for a minute or two."

Knowing that Jake was an interim replacement for Whistler and Tombstone, Dan was worried. Arriving at the building, he saw Masie Skates perched on the edge of a bench in the waiting room, nervously twisting a worn wedding ring. Thin, blonde hair, streaked with slivers of gray, was pulled severely into a knot at the nape of her neck. Lines of care gathered in crowds under her eyes and slowly scattered like fine webbing across her pale cheeks.

As Jake swung through the office door, he motioned her into his office with Dan reluctantly trailing.

"Sorry about Tom," Jake said and coughed self-consciously, trying to ignore her tear-streaked face. "But these tragedies happen every day. Too often, I might add. I'm told that his heart just stopped while he was patrolling the north wall last week."

Masie merely nodded as she sat with feet tucked under the chair and in the uncomfortable silence, a clock began its measured flight of time in shrill notes, striking eleven times while Jake walked to the window, waiting until the clock was silenced, before speaking.

"About the pension, Masie, I noticed that you're not his legal wife," Jake said, looking over her head, eyes on the clock. "Consequently, you're not entitled to any benefits that may be due Tom. I assume you knew that, or is that the reason you're here?"

"I, uh, I thought that after ten years, that is, Tom said that I was a commonplace wife or something like that." Her voice trailed off as she wiped her eyes with a wadded handkerchief.

"Yes, uh," he said, clearing his throat. "You must mean common-law wife. Well, he never filed for a divorce according to our records so that means you have no claim on his pension which goes to his legal wife, if she's living."

During the long pause, both men were concentrating on the scenery outside the window while Masie sniffled and squirmed in the chair. Finally, Jake rose and shuffled some papers on the desk as he said, "There's one more thing. Rumors are circulating about Roller. Was he bringing whiskey inside?"

Masie sat up in the chair and gasped. "No! I never heard anything so awful, saying that about a dead man who can't defend himself."

"You can't take this to heart. It's just another rumor and there's all kinds around these days."

Masie snatched off her glasses, nervously wiping them with the hem of her dress. "If Tom was doing that, I'd have known about it."

"Did he have any extra cash, you know, other than his pay?"

Anger now replaced tears as Masie tugged at the skirt of her faded dress. She laughed bitterly, saying, "Do I look like a woman whose man had extra cash to spend? Look at me!"

"Maybe he was sending his, uh, other, uh, wife, money?'

"Why don't you ask her?" She rose from the chair, marched across the room and through the door, head held high.

"Dealing with employees is far worse than with the damned cons," Jake commented dryly. "It's tough but we have to follow the law."

The morning Masie's body washed ashore was a rare sunny day for November when the weather is always ambivalent about its desires. Assorted waves leapfrogged across the rocky beach, some smashing in with wild abandon while others trailed along in hushed whispers barely rising above the surface.

A lone seal pup flopped and squealed in the surf while nearby, a floating body thought to be its mother, raised a fisherman's curiosity and he waded over to investigate the pup's wild antics. To his horror, long streams of human hair, billowing out from a bloated face, resembling seaweed clinging to a water-soaked log, greeted him as small crabs clung tenaciously to the outstretched legs.

"Found not far from the hotel where she lived." The sheriff said, scratching his head while he stood beside Jake. Dan had just joined them and was told they had been notified because of the body's proximity to the prison.

"Incidentally, the coroner, who just left, says it's impossible to pinpoint the time of death because she was found floating in the bay. He also says the gas from a drowned body that would raise the body to the surface, forms slowly in this icy water. Also, it takes almost two months for the fingernails to loosen and hers seem to be intact."

"Do you have a wild guess?"

"All these clues say she's been in there, maybe a week or two, not longer. Damned thing, though, looks like her eyes were gouged out, probably by fish but that's another conjecture."

"You mean that could have been done before she died?"

The man shrugged, saying, "Don't know. An autopsy will show if she really drowned, by finding sand and debris in her nose, mouth and lungs. If she was killed elsewhere, there would be nothing in her lungs but debris could still be found in the mouth. We'll know more after the autopsy."

Shivering at the implication, Jake cursed and lit a cigarette, hands shaking as he tossed the match.

"She was once a matron at the prison. Maybe it was an act of vengeance by some released prisoner or prisoner's relative." Jake volunteered as he studied the body.

"Doubt it. Too much time has passed since she worked at the Hen House. It could be suicide, though." Jake said, contemplating the sandy shoreline as he tossed the still-burning cigarette into the shallow water lapping the rocks and glanced across the body at Dan who was chewing on a toothpick. "What's your thought, Dan? You were there in the office the day I questioned her about the money."

"She took it pretty hard, I know." Dan was thoughtful as he studied the decomposed body. "But I don't think she showed any suicidal tendencies, just anger."

"Yeah, if you look at her clothing, she wore a heavy coat and in the pockets she had stuffed hundreds of dollars which probably meant that she was going on a trip."

While the men debated the circumstances, an ambulance arrived for the body, much to their relief.

"Well, she's no longer in our hands, thank God," Jake was shaking his head. "She's the coroner's problem now."

Thoughts of Masie and Roller, like specters in a mystery would trouble Dan all evening. Their unexpected deaths plus the odd circumstances related to her drowning, as well as a sudden heart attack in a healthy man, were very disturbing. As Dan walked back to his apartment that evening, memories of a certain incident in Masie's life that had occurred several years before, kept replaying in his mind like a broken Hollywood movie reel, reinforcing the idea that perhaps her death really was a murder. Working at the Hen House had brought Masie into close contact with Freida when she had been incarcerated there.

It had been a morning with heavy mist moistening the ground, clouding the air like fog and dense enough to place the tower guards on alert. Dan had just arrived on the Porch when Messenger arrived, saying, "Loot, got a minute?"

"Okay." Dan walked around his desk. "I was on my way out. What is it that's so urgent?"

"Sir, I found a strange note in the library where I'm working and decided you need to look at it."

Dan struggled to hide his surprise. This prisoner who had been so antagonistic when they first met, was now offering help. As Dan studied the note, Messenger added, "It fell out of a religious book, if that means anything."

After he left, Dan handed the note to Sawbucks. "Does this appear to be any kind of plot?"

Sawbucks read the note slowly, turning over the paper in his hands as he looked across at Dan. "It's hard to say, Dan. What do you think?"

"Well, 0100-1776 means absolutely nothing to me but since Messenger brought it over, I'll take it seriously. That guy is no squealer. So he's apparently showing some gratitude."

"Thank you for what?"

"Thanks for taking him out of the clutches of Whistler, Croaker and that gang, as well as getting him the job in the prison library. He's changed a lot and all for the better."

"So, what you're saying is that even if this means nothing, you want him to think you're taking it seriously."

"No. What I'm saying is that I am taking this note seriously!"

Weeks passed without any incident and just when they decided it wasn't a plot after all, Dan was summoned to the warden's office. Walking into the office, he saw Jake and Whistler were seated by the window with the desk separating them from the others, a man in a ministerial suit, Roller and Masie Skates.

"Come in Dan," Jake rose and shook hands as Dan looked around in surprise, saying, "What's this all about?"

"This is the Reverend Browne," pointing to the man in black and, of course you know Roller and Masie."

Both nodded without smiling as Jake continued, "Well, there's a story here and I guess I'm the one to tell it. Remember that strange note you gave me weeks ago?"

Dan nodded as Jake said, "Well, it was a plot, all right, a devious plot, conceived and carried out by the people in this room."

Masie began sobbing as her husband reached over to comfort her. "She's innocent Jake." Roller spoke in a pleading voice just as Masie jumped up, saying, "No I'm not. I'm as guilty as the others."

"What the hell's going on?" Dan was confused.

"If everyone will be quiet, I'll finish the story. You see, Masie is Freida's matron and conceived a plan to free Freida."

"Ah, Freida." Dan had smiled in remembrance of the notorious woman now sitting on death row for multiple murders. "Go on, I'm anxious to hear this."

"Masie Skates and the pastor here plotted with another prisoner to arrange Freida's pregnancy."

All eyes shifted to Masie who clung to Roller's hand.

"By getting Freida pregnant, she would not be executed for those nine months at least, and by then, what do you think the press and public would say about executing a mother, especially a new one?"

Dan's laugh was high voltage in a room filled with electric tension.

"What's so funny?" Jake's face was now bright red.

"I'll explain when you finish the story."

"They had devised a plan for an inmate to enter her cell in the middle of the night when Masie would disappear for an hour, leaving the door open, returning before the watch changed. The prisoner was a trustee who did kitchen duty and was able to wander around the prison at all hours."

A vague memory came to Dan, like a preview from an old film clip, of a prisoner walking through the yard on the night he had first met Roller who had passed him off as a nut and he wondered if it had been the same convict. At this point, the pastor spoke in a low voice, "I did assist in this plan and I was passing notes in the library. I don't regret my actions because I am a man of God and don't believe in capital punishment for anyone, especially a woman who has the womb of life in her."

"All you needed was a man to cooperate?" Jake had bellowed. "Asking that in here is like asking a kid if he wants to buy a candy store."

"Okay, Dan," Jake smiled. "It's your turn. What's so funny?"

"When Freida was in the Hen House years ago, Croaker happily performed a hysterectomy on her because she'd been complaining about pain. So, Freida can't get pregnant but she did almost get away with the hoax of the century. Besides, having one last go at sex, she probably would be able to stall the execution for several months, gaining the time she needed for the inevitable sympathy created by the press."

There was silence in the room as everyone was lost in contemplation.

"The wording on the note is simple now that we know of the plot. The cell door would be open at one in the morning on July Fourth."

As Dan delved into the past in search of any clue that might explain Masie's eerie death, he remembered the times when Freida reigned, which was a good word for it. Rogers had been notified in advance that a woman was being brought into the prison while awaiting execution.

"All hell will break loose in the press," Rogers had shouted, "when they hear that we're putting her in a cellblock with condemned men."

"So, where the hell do we house the bitch?" Jake was smiling across the desk as Whistler shook his head.

"Have to put her over there on the Cakewalk."

"So, what do we do with the men already there."

"Godammit!" Rogers shouted, nerves already shot by the calls from the press. "What the hell should I do? Put her in the spare bedroom of my home?"

"Good thought," Dan laughed. "But you wouldn't sleep well."

"Yeah," Jake added. "She might accuse you of rape!"

Until a better solution was found, Freida was placed in an unoccupied cell on the top floor. And the cell was made comfortable by a matron, Masie, who lived on the grounds. However, Freida's demands and complaints were endless.

"She wants what this time?" Sawbucks said, yelling into the phone one morning. "No, she can't have a radio or anything else that's been banned for all death row inmates. And if she doesn't like the food, tell her to complain to the cook, not me."

Later, Dan arrived at work to find Masie waiting at his desk. "Need help?"

"Yes, I wanted to see the warden but he's away and I'm told that you can help. The prison chaplain has refused to see Freida on a daily basis because he's so busy with the men. I want to

193

know if it's all right for my own minister in town to come to the prison. Our church would like to adopt Freida, so we'll pay for all the expenses. In fact, I have donated my own salary toward the fund."

Dan shook his head in amazement. "You know Freida has an uncanny ability to make people bend to her will. Do you know her crime and that she's been in here before for the murder of one of her husband's? A third husband who died under mysterious circumstances, I might add."

Masie shook her head. "She's innocent. She was framed before and this death was a total accident. God will save her."

Masie was immediately dismissed and even though her husband was not involved in the plot, Roller was demoted to the night watch on the towers.

The minister was banned from the prison when the board realized there was no evidence that any crime had been committed. Freida kept her date with the gallows, yelling at her executioners, "I'll see you boys later, downstairs!"

Chapter XVIII

San Francisco 1931

It was noon and the church bells in the belfry of Old St. Mary's were pealing for the lunch crowd mingling along the streets of Chinatown where Angel was indulging in his favorite sport. The room in the attic was suffocating, as a sweating Angel continued studying and selecting numbers from a sheet of paper.

"This game of lottery that our neighbors in Chinatown play illegally, by the way, will eventually be a very popular game called *Keno* in Nevada now that gambling has become legalized, the governor of the state announced today," noted the local paper. Leaning on the table, under a horoscope tacked on the wall above, Angel was intently studying the horoscope and contemplating numbers when someone jostled him. Looking up from the paper, he was greeted by Chan.

"Good afternoon," Chan said as he took the paper Angel was reading, crumpled it in his fist and tossed it into a waste basket.

"Now," Angel's face reddened. "Why did you do that?"

Chan smiled and said, "I think we need to have another talk, shyster man."

"Oh. Now what did I do?"

"I'm ready to discuss terms and other matters today." He turned and walked away, glancing back once to beckon Angel with a crooked finger, saying, "Follow me."

195

Sighing heavily, Angel grabbed his briefcase and trailed the rotund figure through the crowded attic, down the stairs and into the import shop below. At the rear of the shop, they pushed through a curtain of beads hanging from the rafters and down another flight of stairs. Here, in the incense-draped bowels of the building, Chan switched on a light and Angel, rubbing his eyes to be sure that he wasn't imagining this scene, opened them to a view of large iron cases encircling the room, containing stacks and stacks of paper money. American money and Chinese money living side by side in quiet harmony spelled millions of dollars squeezed into a dusty moldy basement in rusted iron crates.

"We are a strange people as you have so often pointed out, Mister Angel. So, we do not trust your banks here nor do we trust the banks in other countries. In China, my home, the banks are corrupt, so that leaves very little choice."

"Oh! Why are you showing me this?" Angel felt nauseous. Somehow, this knowledge didn't feel too healthy or hopeful for the survival of Herbert Angel's skin.

Shrugging, Chan looked around the small room that was not much larger than a bank vault. "First, let me explain that the good news of legal gambling has been announced by the governor of our neighboring state. Secondly, I have decided to relocate to Nevada where I can operate with peace of mind."

"Congratulations," Angel said, still feeling queasy. "And what do you want of me?"

"I want you to help me dispose of all this. I read with great interest about the prison inferno that destroyed a large plant. The fire danger in this city is a threat every day for us. Most of the stores are of wood construction and just think what a bonfire this room would make, sir."

"Dispose?" By now, Angel was not only incredulous but something else had just sneaked in during the last few seconds, a sense of fear.

"Yes. Well, you have many contacts here in the city and over, uh, in the, uh, prisons there," gesturing toward the bay. "Perhaps you could meld some clever minds together and come up with a solution as to where to stash my wealth without the government discovering it after I have moved out of Chinatown into Nevada."

Chan leaned back in a rocking chair and lit a cigarette with long fingers that appeared to Angel to be shaking slightly.

Meanwhile, Angel collapsed into a chair which had been teetering under stacks of books which he placed on the floor and shaking so hard, he was forced to place his hands on his knees to steady them. *What the shit! How do I get out of this?* "Uh, I don't have a safe at home and if I did, it couldn't hold this amount."

Chan was smoking and nodding his head. "Yes, but what about those inmates of yours?"

"Indeed. There are some who are very good at breaking into bank vaults. Do you want them to steal this?"

Chan's laugh rose from the bottom of his large belly as he half-rose from the chair, holding onto his stomach and flopping back down. "Ah, sir, you are a wise solon but not very people smart. You think I would trust one of your thieves with my money? No, no! What I want is someone who is capable of designing a vault for me without the knowledge of the police or the government. Then, after transporting the money from here across the state lines, he would build an underground vault over there on my property, with its location known only to me."

"And the trick, sir, is to get it across the state lines without being caught, is that it?"

Angel continued staring at the Chinese man, *wondering how he had become so enmeshed in this old thief's life.*

"So, you're beginning to see the situation, Mister Angel."

Chan rose from the chair, his long queue swinging as he walked over to the crates of money. Reaching inside one, he drew out a handful of large notes and spread them out on a table, saying, "Here's an advance for your use."

"Oh," Angel was shaking his head vehemently, "No, I don't want your money. I'll accept your offer after the deed has been accomplished. Once more, let me go over this. You want me to contact a briefer who's had lots of experience with bank vaults. Have him design and build one over on your Nevada property as well as arrange the transportation of this money out of California and into Nevada without arousing the curiosity of the law. Is that it?"

Chan was smiling broadly as he said, "Indeed. That's it."

Angel was sweating so profusely now that he reached into a pocket for a handkerchief and began wiping a wet brow.

"What will you do with this expert, sir? Are you going to have him killed afterward because of his knowledge?"

"Oh! Indeed, no such thought had entered my mind. I realize that whomever you select will also be a bright industrious man who probably would like to work as a runner or something like that."

"With gambling legalized over there, Mister Chan, you won't have need for runners, remember?"

Chan flushed, saying, "Of course. It's just a terminology that I've become accustomed to using. There would be plenty of jobs for him to fill. After all, in another state, his record would be clean, right?"

"You're wrong there, Chan. When it comes to legal, let me explain. In this country, his criminal record follows him throughout his life wherever he lives."

"Oh," Chan sighed, saying, "That's not true in China."

"In China, and this is not meant to offend, he wouldn't be alive by now, right?"

Without replying, Chan turned toward the door and said, "I will expect to hear from you by this weekend, sir."

As Angel trailed Chan up the stairs and through the store, he heard shouts and laughter from the gaming room above and suddenly had no stomach for gambling.

At the door to the shop, Chan turned and pointed to the church steeples peering through the misty day and said, "Sir, you will go there now and pray?"

Goddamn, Angel thought as he walked along the street, *the man's a mind reader. That's just where I'm going.*

San Quentin Prison

The photoengraving shop and printing press were situated in the basement of the administration building and were very busy recording prisoners' pictures as well as printing the Walled City Journal and many other official papers.

Lefty, also known as Master Key, was a man of many aliases as well as a creature of habit, a habit that forced him to work in the dark, relieving businesses of their money. A tall man with wide-lipped ears and a pronounced lisp, Lefty was the subject of ridicule from his earliest years that eventually drove him to kill his partner in crime who had overstepped their friendship by calling Lefty a faggot. Lefty was doing hard time with little hope of parole for the crime of murder in tandem with safecracking.

When Lefty was informed of a visitor this Saturday morning, he was perplexed. Who the hell wanted to see him? To his surprise, it was his former attorney who had not only lost his case but was erased from his mind forever, so he hesitated before crossing the room and joining Herbert Angel at the table.

Slumping down on a small stool by the table, Lefty smirked. "What the hell do you want? The way you hung me out to dry, why am I even here?"

With that said, Lefty rose, pushing the stool back under the table, saying, "And don't come conning me again, Angel."

Shadows filtering through the barred windows played across his face, weaving and twisting in bizarre patterns as he spoke.

"Wait a minute!" Angel rose from the chair and said, "This is important!"

Then, noticing that the guard perched in the corner had also risen from his chair while grasping a billy club dangling from his waist, Angel smiled and calmly sat back down. Lefty walked back to the table and squinting through narrow eyes, glared at Angel, saying, "What's so damned important?"

"Well," glancing over at the guard, Angel lowered his voice. "Can't we discuss this a little more privately, Lefty?" He was motioning toward the corner where the guard, now leaning back in his chair, was engrossed in a magazine.

"Yeah," Lefty slid back onto the stool. Angel offered a package of Camels which Lefty eagerly grabbed and stuffed into his shirt pocket, eyebrows raised as he shook the package. "Fags all that's in here?"

Angel leaned closer, ignoring the question. "It's worth a lot of money to you even if you can't get out, you'll have lots of spending money in here," winking at Lefty.

"Well, what is it?"

"I need the name of a reliable safecracker."

Lefty threw back his head, laughing, "You?"

"No, not me," Angel nervously looked around at the guard who now appeared to be dozing behind the magazine. "It's for a friend and actually it's a favor I owe. No, it's nothing illegal." Angel was turning over in his head the legality of the situation, pushing away any thought of the terrible consequences from moving scads of illegal, perhaps stolen, tender across state lines.

"If it ain't illegal, why are you here? Can't find an honest man in the city or state? Gotta come in here for that?" Lefty began laughing so hard that he woke the guard who glared over at him.

"Okay," he looked at Angel who was not laughing. In fact he was frowning, *wondering why he was haggling with this crazy con!*

"Let me get this straight, old man. You want me to get you a safer from in here or out there?"

Angel shifted uncomfortably in the chair and hissed, "Outside! How could anyone do it from in here?"

"Well, that's what I asked, for Chrissakes! How would I fit into this scheme? What's in it for me, old man?"

"You provide the man. I'll work with him out there and you'll receive say ten percent of the share, guaranteed."

The men stared at one another, each unsure about the other. "What the hell's this?" Angel was getting agitated and finally said, "You don't trust me, an attorney?"

Six Months Later

"Were you here when Lefty checked in?" Dan was sharing a morning coffee with Sawbucks in the officer's mess.

"No. Why?"

"It's just a nagging hunch. I've noticed that he seems to have lots of cash to spend in the canteen these days."

"Maybe he's from a rich family."

"I don't know. Maybe I should investigate."

That afternoon, Dan went to the basement where the inmate files were stored, some reaching back almost one hundred years. Rummaging through the files developed into a hopeless task and just as he had decided to forget the search, Lefty's name popped up. Leafing through the folder, Dan learned that Lefty had a master's degree from a prestigious university but had been disowned by his family. Further research revealed that they had moved to another state, claiming his criminal activities were embarrassing the family.

"His family divorced him," Dan exclaimed as he sat in the café that evening with Angel, who nervously asked, "Why are you so interested in this con?"

For some reason, Dan hesitated, saying, "Oh, I'm always curious about the men and why they're in here."

Angel laughed and said, "When you find that out, let me know. I could write the book!" His laughter seemed hollow.

Walking home that evening Dan decided that since Lefty was not receiving help from home, it must be coming from another source. Where? Topper? What was he doing for Topper? Suddenly Dan realized with a shiver that he was finally closing in on the elusive Topper.

On the following morning, emerging from the ferry, Dan hesitated for a few tempting moments before Paddy's Saloon on the San Francisco pier, then turned and walked toward a large building several blocks away. It was crowned with three colorful flags billowing in the morning breeze like bright flickering candles on a birthday cake. The clanging trolleys, with bells ringing and overhead wires crackling, rattled and swayed on rusty tracks, added to the aura of the city. It was a welcome change from the grim austerity of the prison atmosphere and Dan stood for a few minutes, savoring the sights and smells of the city sidewalks.

The office reeked of old leather and stale cigar smoke. Papers were scattered across the desk, overflowing over to an adjoining chair and carpeting the floor to the edges of bookcases that papered the wall. It was, in short, an office in dire need of assistance and perhaps, janitorial service, Dan thought, as he closed the door.

The woman behind the desk did not glance up as Dan entered. Bright red hair stacked on top of her head in large round curls like plump, uncooked sausages, held pencils and an extra pair of glasses. She continued tapping the typewriter keys like a pianist intent upon creating a great opus.

An inner door banged open and a tall man, sporting a smile and gray goatee strode across the room, arm extended, greeting Dan and gesturing, "You must be the officer from the prison. I'm Treasury Agent Smythe. Here, come into my office. It's not as cluttered and more private." He was speaking while hurrying along the hall toward a small sunlit office in the rear of the building. "The government doesn't give us much room to work in." He was laughing and pulling up a chair for Dan. Turning to his desk, Smythe opened a folder and said, "This just arrived a few minutes ago, which explains why I was late in meeting you."

"This is Lefty's file?"

"Yes. It seems that he was charged with counterfeiting but the charges didn't stick and he was acquitted by a jury. So, our friend has a history of kiting also."

"Who was his attorney?"

"Let me see," he said, shuffling through some papers. "Ah, here it is. Herbert Angel."

Dan leaned back in the chair, exhaling as he lit a cigarette.

"Now, he was later picked-up on the same charges and found guilty. The plates were actually found in his possession. Only this time, there was a murder charge tacked on. These guys are never smart, despite all their university degrees!"

Reaching into a drawer, the agent withdrew a package, saying, "These are the plates". After handing them to Dan who studied them before replacing them on the desk, he continued. "Anyway, these ten-dollar bills just surfaced on the streets of the city," handing a stack of bills to Dan. "They might as well have his name printed on them. It's his work, all right."

"Well, he's working these days in the prison's photo shop."

Smythe threw back his head, laughing as he said, "They put Lefty in charge of engraving without checking on his past?"

"Yeah, Lefty, the old fox, was placed in charge of the chicken coop! However a check on his past only showed kiting. I have to catch him in the act first but that won't be too hard."

"You're right, they always get caught and this time, Lefty won't have far to go after being sentenced."

This had been a most rewarding day because Dan believed that more than one criminal would be caught.

A few days later, on a stormy evening when the walls of the apartment resembled prison bars, Dan decided to stroll along the beach that rimmed the prison. The storm was fierce, with the surf fuming and foaming as waves roller-coasted across the beach with a thunderous roar. Looking over at the prison, he noticed a light where one shouldn't be at this time of night. Curious, he crossed the sandy beach and approached the front gates.

"Evening, Loot," the guard said with a snappy salute. "Enjoying the storm? It's a lulu."

"I'm going over to my office."

"Want me to call ahead so they won't be surprised?"

"Good idea." Dan saw no point in explaining the mysterious light now. As he approached the administration building, he noticed the light was now extinguished. While quietly surveying the building, he saw three convicts hastily emerge through the basement door and stopping when he turned his flashlight on them.

"Hi, Loot," Lefty said calmly as if he had anticipated this encounter.

"Stand where you are!" Dan ordered, reaching for his whistle.

"Ah, Loot, we were just having a little card game, that's all." Lefty whined while the others remained by his side.

The whistle brought two guards from the building who stared at the group.

"What's up, Loot?"

"Search them and then I want them handcuffed and returned to their cells." Dan, irritated by Lefty's smart-ass attitude, was thinking, *don't address me as an equal!*

"Yessir." One guard started handcuffing Lefty while the other guard grabbed the two shaking prisoners, handcuffing them together.

"Hey, we ain't done nothing!" Lefty shouted.

"For one thing, you're out of your cells during lockup time. Keep it up, Lefty, and you'll be in solitaire for the rest of your sentence!"

"But we got permission."

"From whom?"

"Captain Jake, Loot."

The following day, a surprised Jake agreed. "Yeah, it's true. I gave them permission to work nights for a few days to get caught up on their work. What's all this about?"

"You'll see," Dan said. "Let's go down to the photo shop." As they walked to the basement, Jake was puzzled, saying, "What the hell's going on?"

Inside, in the dim light, it seemed the storm of the past weeks had shredded the room, with boxes and papers in total disarray. Several guards, accompanied by men in dark business suits were busily tearing apart the equipment stored there until some copper plates were found hidden under a supply of paper. Inks, aging materials, rags and ten-dollar bills were discovered, to Jake's dismay.

"Lefty's spending habits at the canteen, were signals that something was wrong. I wasn't sure but I suspected he was spending some ill-gotten gains," Dan said as Lefty kept shaking his head. "Then when the Treasury Department heard there was an engraving shop at the prison, they weren't surprised to discover counterfeit bills suddenly circulating around the state. When I first contacted them about my suspicions, they were surprised to learn that Lefty was in charge of a printing shop."

It was later learned that the supplies were smuggled in by incoming fish and finished bills departed in the hands of parolees. Lefty had another ten years added to his sentence.

"What does this say to anyone curious about inmates?" one guard asked as they walked Lefty back to the cellblock. Another guard, smirking at Lefty said, "Well, it tells me you guys are really stupid. You can be creative and stupid at the same time!"

Lefty, of course, never seeing the error of his ways, laughed at the guards. "Hey, you dumb bulls. I could have had a few thousand bucks set aside for you if you'd been smart!"

The newspapers were merciless in their editorials with stark headlines: "The Great Paper Mill Caper inside prison walls! Go to prison and get rich! The convicts are manufacturing their own money while the taxpayers pay for the supplies and prison official's sleep."

San Francisco

Angel crumpled the newspaper, angrily tossing it into a waste basket by his desk and waited for the telephone to ring. It would only be a matter of days when Chan will send his hatchet men. That stupid Lefty! Couldn't leave well enough alone and had to start printing money again after being warned against it! It was now a question of either losing my license or my life! Or both! Lefty was in a position now to bargain with the government, able to reveal a knowledge of Chan's illegal money and the proposed transportation of it across state lines. Angry that he had confided in Lefty and worried about the consequences, Angel felt betrayed. His penchant for gambling had left him without spare change and there were neither close friends nor relatives to provide a safe haven. Remaining by the window gazing across gray turbulent waters, his thoughts of prison spires beckoned. Of course! Snapping his fingers, Angel knew where he could find refuge. Informer had been keeping in touch on a regular basis through letters and postcards. Angel decided that the young man could probably use a good attorney over there on the coast. Publishers of small newspapers seem to always be subjected to law suits.

Angel left his apartment, hailed a taxi and went to the wharf where he caught the last ferry crossing the bay this evening. In his pocket was a postcard from a small village near Drakes Bay along the coast with a few fishing shacks, a bait shop, a newspaper that printed all the fishing news and an occasional wedding. After his dinner tonight at Witt's End, Angel planned to leave for his new life. In time, Herb would convince Chan to bring his business into Nevada legally.

Chapter XIX

San Quentin Village

Ham Crane sat on a wicker rocker in the screened porch of the old clapboard boarding house and lit a cigar, allowing the smoke to smother the room as he puffed. It was late morning and light filtering through the clouds cast a tarnished glow across the day. Glancing at his watch, he noticed it was time to meander over to the café but for the moment, he was content to quietly remain here. Lately, it seemed that he was living more and more in the past. When he arrived here in the late nineties, the prison became his only home after the death of his wife. It still hurt to remember her and how wonderful life had been with her in those days. That is, until the evening he had returned from the hospital to find his home ransacked and Pearl in a pool of blood on the kitchen floor. That day, as he knelt over the broken body, an empty life ahead flashed before his eyes and a rage consumed his grief, a rage that frightened him, a doctor sworn to preserve life. She had been his one true love and with no children, what was there to live for? At the trial of her killer, Ham gradually discovered a reason to live, attending the trial daily until the man's face and name were graven into his soul. Even now, he smiled at the clever road he had taken that day. Standing over her grave, he made a silent vow: *Pearl, my darling, you have not died in vain. You have shown me the way to another life where I can use my skills as a doctor for the imprisoned.*

Volunteering to serve at the prison hospital he took the warden and the board by total surprise. "You are a well-respected physician," the warden had said, with raised eyebrows. "Why are you giving up your practice to work here for peanuts?"

"I have found my calling, sir," Ham said smoothly. So, in 1898, Ham Crane became the prison physician who would eventually wield more power and prestige than the warden himself. Always vocal about his concern for the prisoners, Ham insisted that the gallows was a wonderful tool. The prisoner should suffer as much or even more than his victim.

"I believe that prisoners are in here to be punished for their crimes and if they must be flogged, that's good. This will deter them from any future crimes. There should be no visitors, no schooling and no play time. The Hole, the Spot and the Gallows will keep our criminals from repeating their heinous crimes." This was part of a speech Ham had given before the state legislature and when he had finished, the applause was thunderous.

After a year of biding his time, Ham made his move. The man seemed too healthy and Ham must first add some small amount of poison to his food, to make his illness look genuine. Then, changing his mind about operating on the man, he decided to dispose of him in the usual way people dispose of vermin.

"Hey, doc," the orderly asked. "What are you doing with the arsenic bottle?"

"Rats in my house, young man. This is the best and quickest way to obliterate them. Didn't you know that?"

"No sir," the orderly said, shaking his head. "Won't it make them sick and make a vomit mess for you?"

"Not if you give them so much they just keel over and die quickly," and pausing, he solemnly added, "But not too quickly."

The authority of the doctor during those early days in the prison was never questioned. The inmate who had died, writhing in agony over a period of two days, was never linked to Ham Crane or his adored Pearl. Even if anyone had become suspicious, the records were so sloppily kept that it would have been impossible to discover this inmate was doing a life sentence for raping and murdering the prison doctor's wife.

Standing over the grave on Boot Hill under the shade of shivering tall eucalyptus trees that provided a chorus with the rustling leaves, Ham Crane watched the prisoners haul the pine box to the cemetery, drop it into a deep hole and shovel clods of wet earth over it. Then, with a smile, he took the carved wooden cross that was to be used as a grave marker and tossed it into a garbage can at the cemetery gate on his way out. *Actually,* Ham thought, *the man was fortunate that he had decided on the arsenic rather than his original plan. Ham had always wondered if it would be possible to remove a man's heart and replace it with an animal heart such as a pig's heart. That sounded like a wonderful experiment. What better guinea pig to use and what better place to perform the gory operation?*

Today, after finishing his cigar and shaking his head sadly, Ham Crane, rising from the chair and clutching his cane firmly in hand, began the trek to the café for his daily nourishment provided by food, friends and fools.

San Quentin Village

Dan was crawling and scratching his way through the fire-blackened debris, scorched hands bleeding while men were pulling him back from the hot ashes of his home.

"Jesus! She's in there with the baby," he screamed as her face, like a pale weeping candle, melted deep within the leaping flames. The incendiary bomb had destroyed the small house and all that remained of his young life, his wife and baby daughter disappeared in the firestorm that raged through the night so long ago. That was the bugle that heralded his departure from the ragged army. No cause on earth was worth the price Dan paid that night.

Tonight, his heart was dancing a wild tattoo as he stumbled through the room searching for the pealing telephone.

"Dan," Sawbucks was yelling into the phone, "They're rais-ing hell in here, banging tin plates on the bars! What can we do?"

"Call up the bugler. That usually works," and Dan replaced the phone, reaching for a cigarette. The dream was so real that his shaking hands couldn't light the cigarette and he walked out onto the porch. The bugler's haunting notes vibrated across the chilly night while Dan remained on the porch until dawn perfo-rated the morning sky.

The day that Dan had eagerly anticipated arrived with cool weather and a line of fish along the porch almost down to the front gates. Dan sighed as he walked past the line of men and wondered if the day would ever come when this fish line would be a thing of the past. Cardoza was seated at Dan's desk, sipping coffee and reading the Walled City Journal while Mouthpiece was pontificating on the reasons for a playground. And so it was that the editor was the first to hear the good news, along with Dan.

"Just to say that we have not only approved the sports program but endorsed my offer as well when I decided to donate that land I have over there by the bay," Cardoza said, laughing.

"Generous," Mouthpiece observed in his dry way. "But, tell me, sir, who would want to live on a piece of ground adjoining this prison?"

In the silent room, a paper rustled as the staff looked in awe at Mouthpiece whose observation was not well received by Car-doza who returned his question with a stony glare.

"This is the best news of my life." Dan quickly broke in and, smiling, shook hands with Cardoza, who seemed more confused than angry at the editor's remark. "I have to contact a friend in the city and make arrangements for equipment and there are schedules to be drawn-up."

Before Cardoza left the office, he turned to Mouthpiece and said, "There are many ranchers in the area who would want that ground, sir. Also, I predict that someday this prison will eventu-ally be torn down."

When the time arrived for dedicating the field, the board received a number of suggestions, among which were Whistler's Folly, Stonehenge, and Rogers Field. When Mouthpiece proposed Loot Field in his editorial, it was overwhelmingly accepted by the prisoners. However, the board decided on Rogers Field. That evening there was a food strike called and when the men were forcibly returned to their cellblocks, tin cups banging on cell bars filled the night air, causing ear-aches and sleeplessness for the guards. On the following morning, it was announced over the speakers that the work crews were to report to Loot Field to begin the landscaping.

Mouthpiece placed the following editorial on the front page of his newspaper with the notation that the article had been penned several years ago by the former editor, Informer:

"From the shadows of the dungeon we emerge into the sunlight of a dusty field. From the tightened lacings of the infamous Overcoat, we now tie the lacings of our athletic shoes and from the shouts of pain in the Stones we hear the shouts of play ball on the athletic field. We salute you, Loot. For those men who luckily were not here during the days of the Overcoat, I will explain that it was an instrument of torture."

An angry Whistler sent a messenger to find Dan, who was busy with Jake arranging a program for the upcoming field meet. The prisoners were now working on building the field, hauling in yards of top soil, concrete and plants as others worked on the new cotton mill with shouts of "When's the games gonna start?" filling the air.

"You're responsible for this!" Whistler was waving a city newspaper as Dan entered the office. "You went over my head. Why wasn't I informed?"

"I guess I did go over your head, in a way. But when I first contacted the Treasury Department, I wasn't sure I had anything, except maybe a hunch."

"I've tolerated your insubordination long enough. You went over my head to get permission from the board for that field and now, this. I think it's time you moved on. I'll arrange for your severance pay and separation immediately!"

211

He turned to the windows and stared across the prison toward the bay, body trembling.

Dan remained standing by the desk while the news of his dismissal sank in. Then, walking toward the door, he looked over at Whistler who refused to turn away from the window, and in a voice that showed no emotion, said, "You have no grounds for my dismissal."

In the cellblocks, the bets were already on over the paper mill caper and whose head would roll but, strangely, Dan's name was never mentioned.

The prison was shrouded in eerie silence while an execution was in progress when Dan walked over to his office to collect personal belongings. The outline of the new stadium was slowly taking shape, emerging through the clouds and silhouetted against the gray sky, harbinger of a better future for the convicts. The storm had abated, tossing only a few teasing showers from the dark clouds scurrying across the skies. A promise of spring was in the air and with that would be the cries of "Play ball!"

Walking away, Dan didn't look back at the gray stone mistress with whom he had shared more than a decade.

The apartment seemed lonelier than ever as he walked out onto the balcony for a smoke. The bay, still a little ruffled after the storm, was slapping the beach playfully and its sighs of contentment could almost be heard above the screeching gulls looking for dinner. A letter from Paddy had been resting on the table for several days and for some strange reason, Dan was reluctant to open it.

Tomorrow he would pack his few possessions and head for another prison where he could almost hear a basketball tapping a backboard. However, Dan decided that tonight belonged to memories and a last dinner with his old friend, Herbert Angel.

Opening the letter as he poured some fresh coffee into a mug, Dan then sat at the table and began reading Paddy's letter. Through the open window, the splashing surf, ebbing and flowing, was the only sound in the room.

At Witt's End, Dan joined Angel, already at their table by the window. Louie brought two mugs of beer, splashing them down on the table with the menu.

"Hey, it's legal now, guys," he said, grinning. "The sheriff can now legitimately consume my home brew."

"How'd he do it before, Lou?"

"How else but with his tail between his legs and an eye on the door!"

"Anything wrong, Dan?" After the laughter in the room subsided, Angel noticed Dan's silence and wondered if Lefty had already been singing.

"Well, you'll hear it later anyway. Whistler fired me today over the counterfeit ring that I exposed. At least that's the reason he gave."

Angel scoffed. "Oh hell, he's so eaten with jealousy over your popularity with the board, he'll look for any excuse to move you out of his way, Dan. Remember they haven't selected the new warden yet."

"Maybe, but I believe it's that I got the field and my recreation program approved by the board with the help of the legislature. Remember when I said that the rivalry between Whistler and Stone would help me. Well, it was Stone who backed me with the board. Boy, that sure rankled the hell out of Whistler!"

Ham Crane walked through the door, cane tapping as he limped toward their table.

"Well, he seems jovial tonight. He must have heard about your dismissal." Angel said as he watched Crane pull a chair toward their table.

"I think I'm closing in on Topper," Dan said as calmly as if he were announcing a baseball score while watching the reactions of his table companions.

Angel laughed but Crane, staring in disbelief, asked, "Why do you need to know him? It's a better institution today than in the old days before the convict-boss system." Then, he hastily added, "If there even is such a character."

"The only time I have ever agreed with you, Crane." Angel said, turning a serious face toward Dan. "There's a good system

213

here and it shouldn't be disturbed. Anyway, I think this Topper guy is really just a myth to keep the cons in line, you know."

"How can you say that it's a good system when the murder of a guard is ordered? When the warden's life is threatened and when an inmate is executed for a crime he didn't commit? All of this is a result of the convict-boss system that you say is so good." Dan said and angrily crushed a cigarette in the ashtray on the table.

Ham Crane was nodding in agreement. "All of this may be true but remember there could have been many more deaths of both guards and inmates without the boss system, myth or not." Then, cocking his head to one side and looking over at Dan, asked, "Do you suspect that I'm Topper?"

Replying with a serious expression, Dan looked at Ham and said, "I can't say yet but I do have my suspicions. When I sat in someone's office one day, I noticed a small statue of three monkeys see no evil, hear no evil, speak no evil. Now, I can't remember where I was that day but I remember that Walrus had his ear sliced off, Masie had her eyes gouged out by someone or something and Auditor had his tongue deliberately sliced off." Pausing for a breath, he added, "As for Bluebeard's death, which doesn't fit any pattern, I think it was tied in somehow, as if to say, see no evil, speak no evil, hear no evil and I would add-don't squeal!"

Lighting another cigarette, he said, "I think that Walrus was murdered on orders from Topper to appease the inmates who were probably becoming restless over this guard. Remember they were already angry over the death of a young con on the Spot which happened before I came here but it was a subject discussed at the time by the guards who lived in fear of retaliation. Even though it was later proven that the Auditor died of an overdose of morphine which I'm sure was given by an inmate, his death was attributed to the guards."

"Good theory," Angel said, nodding. "But I believe the inmates took care of that sadist, Walrus, in their own way. And, I might add, without any help from a mysterious prison boss."

"Bags was also murdered," Dan said, ignoring Angel's remark, "on Topper's orders because he was going to reveal the

Christmas escape plans. He left that Greek story on my desk because he thought we were going to be taken hostage."

"No, no," Angel said, shaking his head. "I think Bags committed suicide. Why? That I don't know, except maybe he thought he would be the target once they got outside."

"Well, he took the names of the others in the plot to his grave." Dan said and waited for several minutes while each man remained lost in thought.

"Okay," Dan said, "to continue with my theory and moving on to Canary's death. I agree it was a strange death and I'm unable to disprove Croaker's theory that it was Canary's heart because he was cremated. And that fact led me to think that maybe Croaker was either Topper or just an evil man. He's still around, you know, living nearby." Dan looked around the table for someone to speak and when that didn't happen, continued with his theories. "Willie's confession was phony but maybe he was ordered to confess, for the very reasons he gave me. Someone had to die to atone for Walrus's murder."

Angel scoffed, saying, "Willie was the actual killer of Walrus and why he said otherwise, confuses me. Maybe he wanted you to think better of him, Dan."

"Well, I'm not convinced that Willie killed Walrus. He wasn't a killer, just look at his record." Dan was unmoved by Angel's argument. "Moving on to Masie, I think she somehow discovered Topper's identity and was murdered to keep her silence. Someone was providing money for Tom to bring contraband into the prison and that accounts for the wads of money found in her coat pockets after she had vehemently denied having any money to live on."

"All wrong, Dan. Masie couldn't live without Tom. And I think the fish got to her which has never been proven otherwise. That coroner isn't the best, you know."

"Then where did she get all that money?" Dan looked at Angel as he sipped the beer. "Anyway, I suspect Tom was dealing in contraband by providing liquor to the cons. But that can't be proven either. Also, I think Sparky was ordered to set that fire and his death might have been accidental. We'll never know."

"I can't argue with that, Dan," Angel agreed as he lit a cigar, the heavy rich aroma invading the diner.

"About Bluebeard," Dan persisted, "I believe he was murdered for the same reason Masie met her death. He was going to reveal Topper's identity."

"Why would he reveal Topper's identity? He had nothing to gain and he was going to die anyway. So, what's the big deal?" Crane looked puzzled.

"You're wrong. He had a lot to gain. He wanted a movie made of his life and promised to reveal Topper's name."

"That's a wild story and I don't believe you," Crane scoffed. "How could you promise a movie of his life?"

"I didn't. I just promised that I would get a reporter in for an interview. That's all he wanted."

"Well, it was a strange death but easy enough to do, just shove enough of those pliant sticks down his throat and," Angel suddenly stopped as his eyes lit up, "the mouth was sown-up by a professional!"

Silence pulled up a chair and joined the party as Crane and Dan stared at Angel whose face was flushed as he said, "a doctor! But who in here has a medical degree?"

Angel leaned back in the chair, a smug look on his face as he inhaled the cigar and the tense atmosphere.

"Easy to find out, isn't it? Just go through thousands of records for a con or a guard with a medical past." Dan chuckled, saying, "That would take months, even years. Also, weren't you a doctor at one time, Ham?"

It was Crane's turn to flush as he said, "Actually I was a doctor here in the early years but I gave up the practice of medicine years ago. I suppose with all the modern medical knowledge of today, I would have to return to school and start all over."

Angel glanced across the table, surprised. "Well, I never knew that. I always thought you were an officer of some sort." Then, he added, "Why isn't there a record of your service here?"

Crane shrugged, saying, "Suppose there is, somewhere." His voice trailed off as he lit a cigarette with shaking fingers. *Futile*

216

to dredge up the past, wasn't it? What could possibly be gained by the state other than a murder conviction meted to an old man for snuffing out a killer years ago? However, there is no time limitation on murder which was reason for concern.

Ignoring his companions, Dan continued pursuing his theories on the mysterious deaths that had been puzzling him for years. "Also, it could be one of the prison personnel with a grudge. Bluebeard was not a popular character by any means."

"What about the orderlies in the hospital? Couldn't they have learned certain procedures over the years?" Angel asked as Crane smirked, "Hell, they only empty bed pans and most are too stupid to learn anything like suturing."

"That's not true," Dan said, looking across at Crane. "That's the trouble when most prison personnel think like that. Just because a man is incarcerated doesn't imply that he's retarded, you know. Getting back to Auditor who, it was rumored, kept a diary which no one has been able to find. In that diary, I think he may have revealed Topper's identity and listed all the deaths attributed to that man over the years. I heard that he planned to use the diary for a book after he was paroled which would be his ticket to fame and fortune. Somehow, this information could have reached Topper who ordered the mutilation in such a bizarre way that it would certainly influence any other potential writer."

"You know, Dan, all these deaths occurred during your watch, and it naturally bothers you. Well, you can't be a god-father to everyone. These people were strange characters and deserved to die, one way or another."

"Well, I've found the deaths puzzling, like a festering sore," Dan replied.

Chapter XX

O n his walk home that evening, Dan reflected on Angel's words and their friendship while still contemplating Crane's role in the scheme of things. At the apartment, he reached for a bottle of whiskey, poured a shot and went out to the deck where he reopened the letter from Paddy.

"Danny: I should have told you the instant you arrived in the city but I was so pleased to know that you survived and saw how well you looked, after such a tragic ordeal. Unfortunately, the other day I was faced with a decision when I accidentally met an old cellmate in Chinatown which reminded me that I do owe you an explanation for my actions. That week of hell began with the formal surrender of our army when we were led like criminals into that filthy rat-infested prison. When our commander complained that we were prisoners of war and were to be treated as such, we were scorned, spit upon and beaten bloody before being thrown into cells. The only sounds we heard were the rifle shots from the execution squad out in the yard there. One by one, the lads were led down the path past our cells and into the yard of death where each evening for a week, we smelled the smoke from the burning pyres. When I seized the chance to escape, I took it. Sure, we took a soldier with us as hostage. It was during this hostage-taking that I heard of the execution of Saemus, ordered in retaliation for our escape. The hostage was released unharmed, thanks be to God, but I never dreamed that Saemus would be put to death for our deed, Mother of God! I continued on my voyage to America and a new life. I am proud of our friendship and would do anything to help you because I remember all the kind deeds you did for the

218

lads who were in prison during that time. It must have been difficult to see the sad ones who went on those hunger strikes, dying to protest their wrongful incarceration and the miserably filthy prison conditions. Your nursing skills saved many lives and, once again, you are in a position to help your fellow man. Now, I give the reason for this letter. Since this gaol mate knows I'm here, I feel it wise to return home to face the courts and clear my name if only for the history books, which will follow. Lastly, I want to again congratulate you for achieving your goal of sports for the prisoners. Yours in Christ, Peadar."

You once asked what happened that long-ago day in the prison, Paddy, Dan was thinking. For some moments, he was back in that filthy prison, face pressed against a sweat-soaked mattress, deafening the sounds of the bullets that took Saemus's life. After spending hours with Saemus, treating his festering wounds, Dan watched him led away to become cannon fodder, never sure what the charges were. Now he knew!

Dan placed the letter in his pocket, lit a cigarette and remained on the porch watching the city lights across the bay vie with the twinkling porch lights of the heavens, feeling lonelier than ever.

San Quentin Village

"Hey, Loot!" Angel called from his car parked by Dan's apartment building. "Can I give you a lift? It's apiece from here." The morning was chilly with a stiff wind blowing off the bay, stripping the tree branches bare.

Dan smiled at the memory, saying, "Yeah, it's apiece from the rest of the world, too."

Dan was surprised to see Angel. He had been in San Francisco for a few days saying goodbye to Paddy and discussing their futures. This time with Paddy was good because Dan was able to understand his friend's desertion mixed with feelings of disillusionment over the entire rebellion. He walked down the stairs after stashing the key under the door mat, suitcase in hand and joined Angel at the curb.

"What's your plan now?" Angel was looking intently at the road as they drove away from the prison.

"I've given it a lot of thought and decided to go to the capitol and plead my case. I can't leave those men in Whistler's or Stone's hands."

"Are you pleading wrongful termination?"

"Something like that, I guess."

"I'll be happy to represent you, Dan. No charge."

Dan laughed, saying, "Appreciate the offer but it would look better if I walked in there alone. Thanks anyway."

"You're right, of course. It would look strange having the prisoner's advocate representing you." His tone was biting with sarcasm.

The drive to the train station was completed in silence with each man deep in thought.

In the breezy morning, leaves were falling, carpeting the sidewalk as Dan approached the depot. Some people were already clustered along the sidewalk waiting for the train whose whistle was heard in the distance.

Dan and Angel shook hands. "Lots of luck, Loot. We'll miss you, the boys and I," said Angel as he turned away, walking to the car where he stood for several minutes studying Dan who never looked back. Saying goodbye was not one of Dan's strong points, always feeling ashamed of his tears. *A weakling, his father would scream at him over the sound of the whip.*

At this moment, Jake and Sawbucks drove up, waving their arms frantically. "Hey, Dan, wait!"

"Come to see me off?"

"Hell, no! We got a mess back there and need you!"

"You forget that I've been dismissed."

Grabbing Dan's arm and suitcase, Sawbucks said, "My car is here and I have the board member, Cardoza and Agent Smythe with me. We're here to get you reinstated."

On the trip to the prison, Jake explained, "There's thousands of men, Dan, milling around the big yard. It started last night with another riot in the mess hall over wormy bread and God only knows what else they've got in their craw! Then, back in the cells they continued banging those goddamned tin plates against the bars all night long. The watch is on edge, nerves jangled, tempers flaring which could mean an accidental shooting. They want better food and won't break the strike unless we promise better conditions in the mess hall and less crowded cells. Now, with your disappearance, the rumors are that athletics will be taken away. They've been on strike all day, refusing to return to the cellblocks and won't eat. We called the sheriff, and the governor's ready to send in troops, if necessary. Goddammmit we've got our guards on the walls armed with rifles and they still won't move."

"What do you want me to do?" Dan's thoughts returned to that rat-infested prison in the old country and the men who died of starvation. "You can't make men eat!"

"Put on your uniform and talk to them. They also want you back and maybe we can appease them with that for a while. After that, we'll take another look at their food. We have a loudspeaker set up in the front office."

"I don't need the front office," he said as they drove through the front gates.

When Dan entered the Porch area, the few remaining inmates working in the gardens turned and with curious eyes, watched him walk steadily toward the big yard. The gates leading from the Porch area opened and all eyes turned in that direction as Dan strode through and into the big yard, weaponless. There were thousands of men backed against the walls, a heavy pall of cigarette smoke draped the yard, curtaining off any fresh air. The silence was deafening as all eyes riveted on Dan, in uniform, smoking a cigarette and calmly appraising the situation.

Overhead on the walls, armed guards pointed rifles in the prisoners' direction while a line of officers armed with clubs was strung along the opposite walls. As Dan walked slowly past the line of guards, he nodded a greeting and they responded with a salute, almost simultaneously. The convicts watched this exchange of greeting with intense looks. Dan strolled over toward the leaders, stood looking at them for several minutes, then turning his back, walked toward the north wall and made a pass with his arm, a wave, signaling lockup.

Once, twice, he repeated this move until the solid wall of men began to move. Slowly at first, then gaining momentum, the inmates returned to their cellblocks to be counted and locked-down. An enormous sigh of relief was audible that evening, some said it was just the bay waters slithering along the sandy beach but others said it was all the men, prisoners and guards, breathing a collective sigh.

In the warden's office, Whistler, Stone, Jake, Smythe, Sawbucks and Cardoza were waiting for Dan. In a scene strangely reminiscent of his first encounter as a fish bull on the carpet years ago, Dan stood by the door and faced his adversaries. Whistler, face a study in controlled white-hot anger, said, "Well, that was quite a display. Was it rehearsed?"

"Whatever that means," Cardoza said, "is insignificant to a most laudatory display of respect for a prison official that I have ever witnessed in my life or ever hope to. Congratulations, Dan, or rather, Loot, as you are known to the men in here. We are all looking forward to the new program of sports that you have arranged."

Dan remained by the door, quietly smoking a cigarette, still confused about his presence here. "Well, I'm not sure of my status today. Am I an employee or not?" He was looking over at Whistler who turned away.

Jake and Sawbucks were both grinning when Jake said, "Your name has been proposed for warden, Dan. Whistler has agreed to resign."

Surprised, Dan glanced quickly over at Whistler who had turned his back to the group, staring through the windows at the twilight slowly descending upon the prison.

"This is a surprise and I'll need some time to mull over this."

"Take your time," Cardoza said, smiling. "Say, until tomorrow."

As they walked down the steps, Dan stopped, saying, "I've no place to go since I gave up the apartment."

Jake laughed. "No, you didn't. Sawbucks and I re-leased it for you. So, here's your key."

"You assumed a lot," Dan said, taking the key.

"Ah Dan, we both know you too well. You would never leave without a fight."

In his apartment that night, Dan unpacked and replaced his few possessions, including the picture of his wife and tiny daughter whose faces were the last he looked upon each night.

On the following morning, the sun tripped over a cloud in its eagerness to rise, disappearing for a few hours and casting long shadows across the bay. Dan was deep in thought as he walked toward the warden's house where the board meeting was scheduled.

"I want to thank you for the honor you have bestowed on me but I have to refuse. It would take me away from the prisoners and they're why I'm here. Thanks again."

The board appointed Jake as the new warden of the state's largest prison over Stone's loud objections.

"Mister Stone, this appointment is our decision. If you want to tender your resignation now, we will accept it."

With a look of constipation, Stone replied, "First, I must know what position I will have here in the future."

"You'll just be a hired guard, sir."

Stone rose and said, "No thanks. I've had better offers in Nevada."

"Then, good luck, sir."

After the door slammed, the board reinstated Dan as the athletic director and Sawbucks continued as officer of the day on the Porch.

Before they adjourned, each board member walked over and shook hands with Dan, congratulating him on the progress he had made in the years he had been at the prison. In one way, they were saying that his dream of easing the harsh conditions prevailing at the prison during that time, had finally come true.

As if in agreement, the sun suddenly burst through the clouds just as the noon whistle blew and the rattle of pots and plates joined in the chorus of male voices. *All was right with the world*, Dan thought, walking toward his new office near the recreation field.

Angel was sitting by Dan's desk, puffing on a cigar and reading the prison paper. "It says here you broke-up the largest strike in the prison's history, Dan. Famous!"

"If you call that fame, then I guess I'm famous. What are you doing here? I thought we already said goodbye."

"Well, you're not leaving so I guess we'll see more of each other, right?"

"Wrong. As a friend I'm asking you to keep away from this prison in the future. If you don't, I may have to take some drastic action, Herb. I can't prove that you're Topper but I have my suspicions. I know that even if you claim that Topper helped relations between the men and the guards, some people were murdered, including your own bad boys."

Angel rose from the chair, shoving it back against the wall and said, "You're right, you can't prove a damn thing! And I'm sorry you are so mistaken about me but I won't hold it against you."

"What's with Angel?" Sawbucks asked a few weeks later. "I never see him anymore."

"Well, he decided to retire. I understand he moved north along the coast, enjoying his retirement working on Informer's newspaper and I also heard that he was co-owner of a Chinese restaurant in Reno, of all places!"

"Why is it that the good people always seem to leave us and the bad apples stay?"

"When you find out, let me know. I could write the book." Dan laughed, quoting his old friend.

A few weeks later, Dan received a call from Jake's office regarding some baseball equipment recently donated to the prison. It was a still-life day as he walked toward the warden's office. Even the trees were barely breathing.

"Come in," Jake called out at Dan's knock. "I'm still trying to get settled in here. Whistler left a lot of junk and I gotta pack it up and send it off to him."

"Where is he now?"

"Oh, directing some prison across the country in his own inimitable way." Jake said, busily packing books when Dan spied the statue of the three monkeys on the desk. *This was where he had seen it before, in the warden's office!*

"Is that yours?" he asked, picking it up and turning it over in his hand.

"Oh. Hell, no. It was Whistler's, maybe Rogers' before him and I saw Croaker with it once. Some con made it. Really good carving, don't you think? All carved from one piece of walnut wood."

Dan remained silent, rubbing his finger across the smooth wood. "What prison did you say he was working in?"

"Oh, don't know, but I can find out for you."

"No. I may contact him later." Dan placed the statue on the desk and turned away, then pausing, added, "Oh, by the way, what's this about donated baseball equipment?"

Chapter XXI

San Quentin Prison

A golden evening hitch-hiked across the sky, pausing briefly to allow a lone goose find its way home before dipping into the inkwell of the night. It was the evening before the grand opening of the new athletic field and Dan walked over to the north wall to survey it for the first time. For months the prisoners had labored long and hard, transporting rich top soil, planting grass and landscaping the area as well as raising the field five feet which attested to the enormous amount of earth they had moved. A bronze plaque bearing Dan's name and bust was installed and the months spent toiling on this field was their thanks for the Loot's many years of struggle on behalf of the inmates. Tonight while he stared at the amazing feat the prisoners had accomplished, Dan brushed away a stubborn pang of homesickness.

The opening day of the first Field Meet held on the new recreation field was accompanied by widespread publicity with several famous sports figures agreeing to attend. Even the weather, usually ambivalent with its moods in September, decided to slough off its grumpy manners and send a brilliant sun rocketing across the blue skies.

In one corner of the field, a baseball team was warming up. Dan's Black Sox were playing a team from the city and the inmates in the crowded bleachers were already placing bets.

In another corner, Benny's boxing team, muscles gleaming and glistening in the sunlight, were lined along the ropes of the ring like anxious gladiators while wrestling teams waited in the wings, eager to flex their muscles.

The relay teams were already on the oval track. Because it was opening day, a popular baseball legend was autographing some baseballs for the men before he walked onto the field with Dan. To his surprise, it took a few minutes to realize that the standing ovation was not for him but for Dan. All the prisoners stood and, with wild hand-clapping, hooting, whistling and stomping feet erupting into a thunderous applause, shouted his name over and over, resounding across the fields and distant hills, "Loot, Loot, Loot!"

For a few moments, Dan stood, waving his cap in quiet acknowledgment as he grinned and then turned, signaling with a wave of his arm for the games to begin.

Epilogue

Informer was awarded the Pulitzer Prize for his expose on the treatment of the criminally insane in the prison system.

Mouthpiece, the charming news editor, remained in prison until his sudden death in the prison hospital of a burst appendix.

Herbert Angel was co-owner with Informer of the newspaper The Coast Crier. He also became co-owner of a very popular Chinese restaurant, The Pagoda.

Nick, the Filipino prisoner, was returned to his homeland prior to World War II where he was involved in the largest bank heist in the history of the Philippines just before World War II.

Fetcher was a gate attendant until his death which was widely covered in the press, becoming known as the only man who ever refused to leave prison.

Ham Crane's body was found sprawled across a grave on Boot Hill. Death attributed to "old age."

Whistler became a warden at an institution in the state of New York where he was taken hostage and murdered during a prison riot over removing sports from prison.

Dan continued as athletic director at the prison until his death when the prisoners observed a minute of silence for the man they called *The Loot*.

Topper, the prison boss, remains a mystery to this day but rumor has it that he still walks the yard at the prison. Night guards have reported strange sightings of a man walking the north wall, trailed by puffs of smoke and a faint whistling sound.

CPSIA information can be obtained at www.ICGtesting.com
Printed in the USA
LVOW081604170112

264296LV00002B/23/P